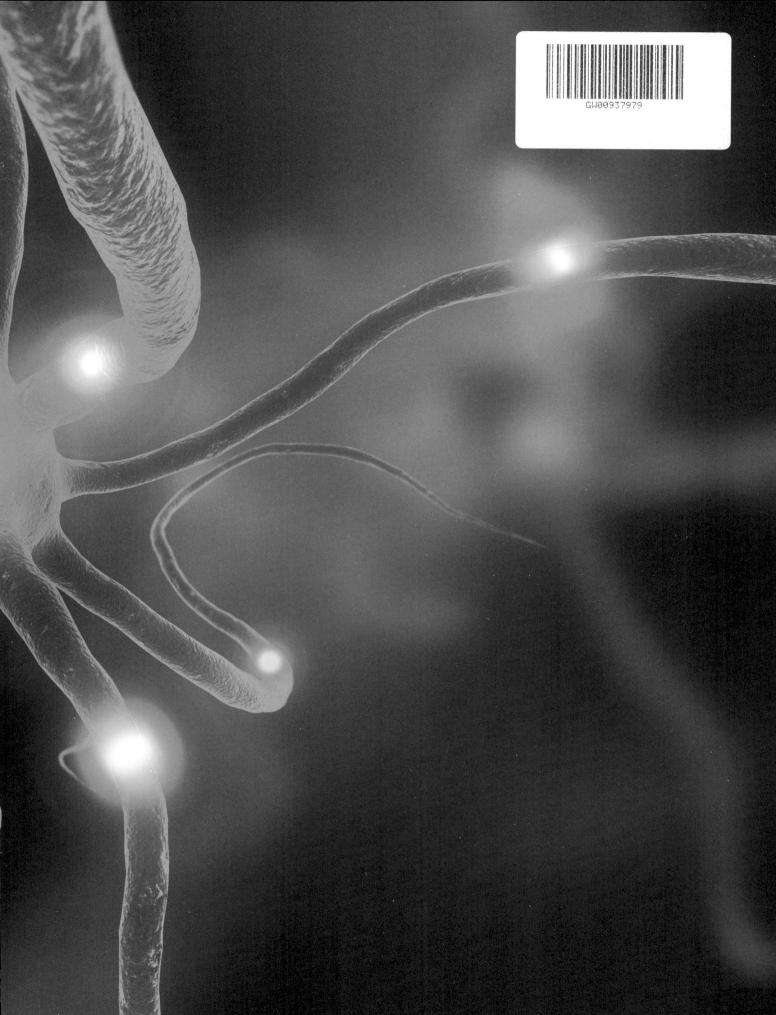

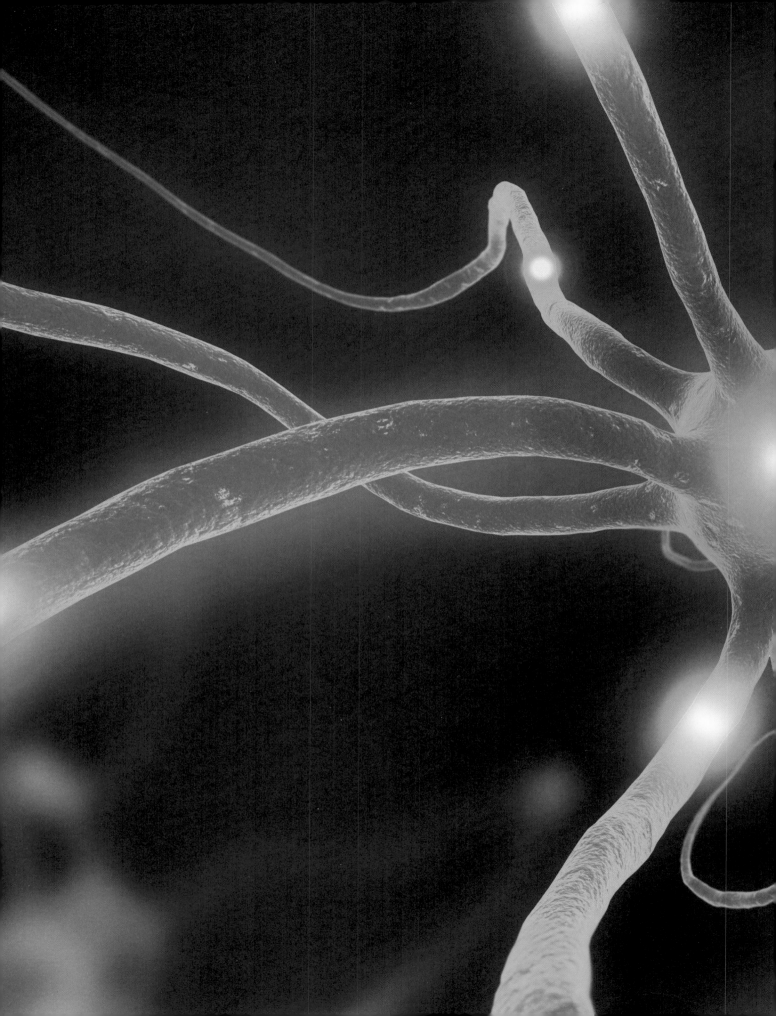

WILD ABOUT
Science

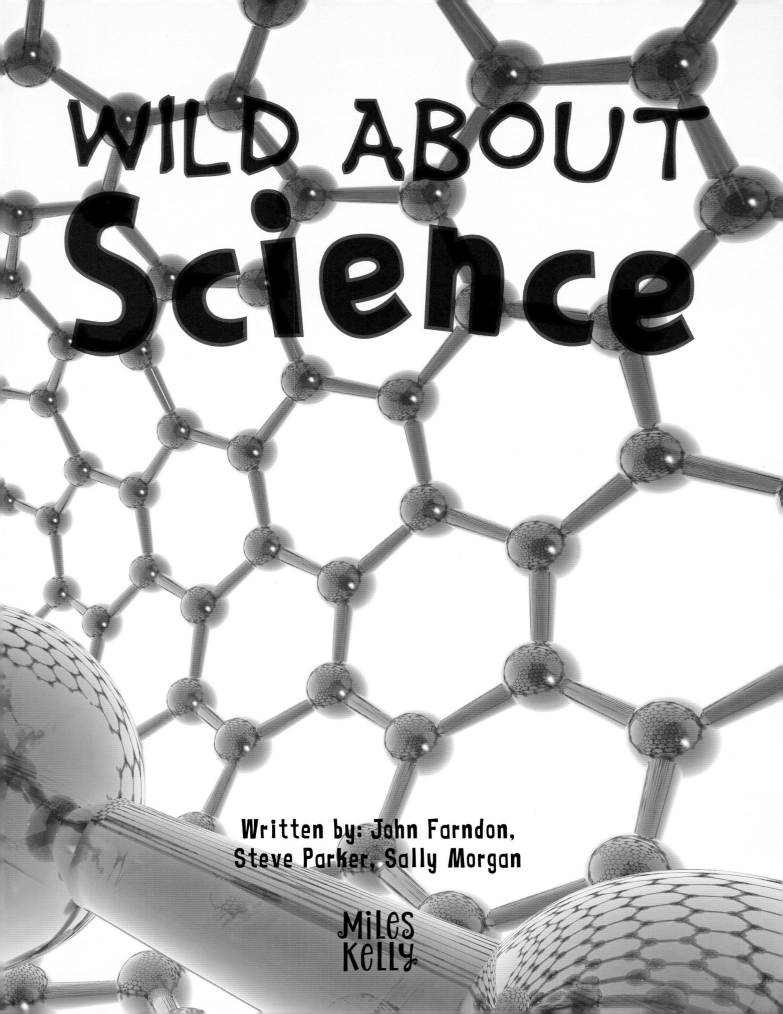

WILD ABOUT
Science

Written by: John Farndon,
Steve Parker, Sally Morgan

MiLeS
KeLLy

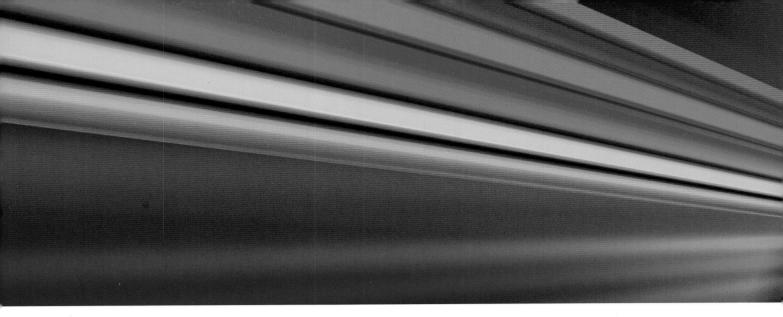

First published in 2017 by Miles Kelly Publishing Ltd
Harding's Barn, Bardfield End Green, Thaxted, Essex, CM6 3PX, UK

This edition printed 2018

2 4 6 8 10 9 7 5 3

Publishing Director Belinda Gallagher
Creative Director Jo Cowan
Editorial Director Rosie Neave
Senior Editors Fran Bromage, Sarah Parkin
Cover Designer Joe Jones
Designers Kayleigh Allen, Joe Jones, Andrea Slane
Image Manager Liberty Newton
Production Elizabeth Collins, Caroline Kelly
Reprographics Stephan Davis, Jennifer Cozens, Thom Allaway
Assets Lorraine King

Consultants Peter Riley, Dr Kristina Routh MB ChB, Clint Twist, Steve Parker

ISBN 978-1-78617-337-9

Printed in China

British Library Cataloguing-in-Publication Data
A catalogue record for this book is available from the British Library

Made with paper from a sustainable forest

www.mileskelly.net

Contents

SCIENCE

1 Even one hundred books like this could not explain all the reasons why we need science. Toasters, bicycles, mobile phones, computers, cars, light bulbs – all the gadgets and machines we use every day are the results of scientific discoveries. Houses, skyscrapers, bridges and rockets are built using science. Our knowledge of medicines, nature, light and sound comes from science. Then there is the science of predicting the weather, investigating how stars shine, finding out why carrots are orange…

▼ In a big city, science is all around you — everything from sky-scraping buildings to speedy vehicles and useful gadgets is based on science and technology.

Machines big and small

2 **Machines are everywhere!** They help us do things, or make doing them easier. Every time you play on a seesaw, you are using a machine. A lever is a stiff bar that tilts at a point called the pivot or fulcrum. The pivot of the seesaw is in the middle. Using the seesaw as a lever, a small person can lift a big person by sitting further from the pivot.

▶ On a seesaw lever, the pivot is in the middle. Other levers have pivots at the end.

Thread

▶ Turning a screw moves it along with more force than the effort used to turn it.

3 **The screw is another simple but useful scientific machine.** It is a ridge, or thread, wrapped around a bar or pole. It changes a small turning motion into a powerful pulling or lifting movement. Wood screws hold together furniture or shelves. A car jack lets you lift up a whole car.

4 **Where would you be without wheels?** Not going very far. The wheel is a simple machine, a circular disc that turns around its centre on a bar called an axle. Wheels carry heavy weights easily. There are giant wheels on big trucks and trains and small wheels on rollerblades.

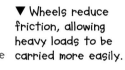

▼ Wheels reduce friction, allowing heavy loads to be carried more easily.

Axle

▼ Two pulleys together reduce the force needed to lift a heavy girder by one half.

5 **A pulley turns around, like a wheel.** It has a groove around its edge for a cable or rope. Lots of pulleys allow us to lift very heavy weights easily. The pulleys on a tower crane can lift huge steel girders to the top of a skyscraper.

▲ Bicycle gears mean you can pedal at the same speed, with the same force, when climbing up a hill or speeding down it.

Reversing gears

Sliding rack

Pinion gear

Bevel gears

Slow pinion gear

Screw-shaped worm gear

▲ Gears change the turning direction of a force. They can slow it down or speed it up – and even convert it into a sliding force (rack and pinion).

Pivot

Lever

I DON'T BELIEVE IT!

A ramp is a simple machine called an inclined plane. It is easier to walk up a ramp than to jump straight to the top.

6 **Gears are like wheels, with pointed teeth around the edges.** They change a fast, weak turning force into a slow, powerful one – or the other way around. On a bicycle, you can pedal up the steepest hill in bottom (lowest) gear, then speed down the other side in top (highest) gear.

When science is hot!

7 Fire! Flames! Burning! Heat! The science of heat is important in all kinds of ways. Not only do we cook with heat, but we also warm our homes and heat water. Burning happens in all kinds of engines in cars, trucks, planes and rockets. It is also used in factory processes, from making steel to shaping plastics.

▲ A firework burns suddenly as an explosive, producing heat, light and sound. The 'bang' is the sound made by the paper wrapper as it is blown apart.

Heat from the drink is conducted up the metal spoon

8 **Heat can move by conduction.** A hot object will pass on, or transfer, some of its heat to a cooler one. Dip a metal spoon in a hot drink and the spoon handle soon warms up. Heat is conducted from the drink, through the metal.

9 **Heat moves by invisible 'heat rays'.** This is called thermal radiation and the rays are infrared waves. Our planet is warmed by the Sun because heat from the Sun radiates through space as infrared waves.

TRUE OR FALSE?

1. Burning happens inside the engine of a plane.
2. A device for measuring temperature is called a calendar.
3. Heat rays are known as infrablue waves.

Answers:
1. True 2. False 3. False

◄ Metal is a good conductor of heat. Put a teaspoon in a hot drink and feel how quickly it heats up.

10 Burning, also called combustion, is a chemical process. Oxygen gas from the air joins to, or combines with, the substance being burned. The chemical change releases lots of heat, and usually light too. If this happens really fast, we call it an explosion.

▲ A burner flame makes glass so hot it becomes soft and bendy, so it can be stretched, shaped and even blown up like a balloon.

11 Temperature is a measure of how hot or cold something is. It is usually measured in degrees Celsius (°C) or Fahrenheit (°F). Water freezes at 0°C (32°F), and boils at 100°C (212°F). We use thermometers to take our temperatures. Your body temperature is about 37°C (98.6°F).

▶ This thermometer contains alcohol coloured by a red dye. As it warms, the alcohol expands (takes up more space). It moves up the thin tube, showing the temperature on the scale.

12 Heat moves through liquids and gases by convection. Some of the liquid or gas takes in heat, gets lighter, and rises into cooler areas. Then other cooler liquid or gas moves in to do the same and the process repeats. You can see this as 'wavy' hot air rising from a flame.

▶ Hot air shimmering over a candle is a visible sign of the heat being convected away.

Engine power

13 Imagine having to walk or run everywhere, instead of riding in a car. Engines are machines that use fuel to do work for us and make life easier. Fuel is a substance that has chemical energy stored inside it. The energy is released as heat by burning or exploding the fuel in the engine.

Turbines squash incoming air

▼ A jet engine has sets of angled blades, called turbines, that spin on shafts.

Jet fuel is sprayed into the air inside the chamber, creating a small explosion

Burning gases spin exhaust turbines

14 Most cars have petrol engines. An air and petrol mixture is pushed into a hollow chamber called a cylinder. A spark from a spark plug makes it explode, which pushes a piston down inside the cylinder. This movement is used by gears to turn the wheels. Most cars have four or six cylinders.

15 A diesel engine doesn't use sparks. The mixture of air and diesel is squashed in the cylinder, becoming so hot it explodes. Diesel engines are used in machines such as tractors that need lots of power.

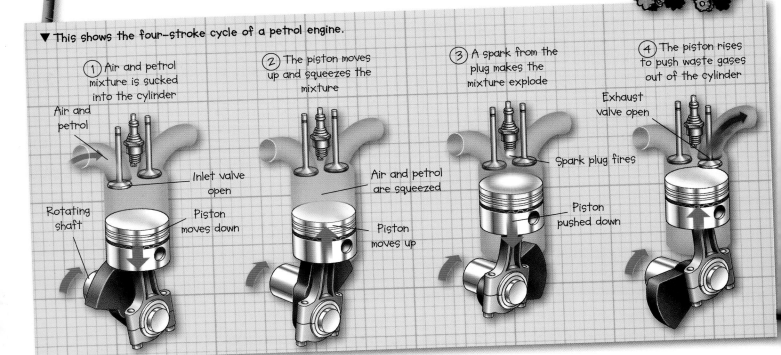

▼ This shows the four-stroke cycle of a petrol engine.

① Air and petrol mixture is sucked into the cylinder

Air and petrol

Rotating shaft

Inlet valve open

Piston moves down

② The piston moves up and squeezes the mixture

Air and petrol are squeezed

Piston moves up

③ A spark from the plug makes the mixture explode

Spark plug fires

Piston pushed down

④ The piston rises to push waste gases out of the cylinder

Exhaust valve open

▲ On a fast jet plane at full power, the exhaust gases from the engines glow almost white-hot.

16 A jet engine mixes air and kerosene and sets fire to it in one long, continuous, roaring explosion. Incredibly hot gases blast out of the back of the engine. These push the engine forward – along with the plane.

17 An electric motor passes electricity through coils of wire. This makes the coils magnetic, and they push or pull against magnets around them. The push-pull makes the coils spin on their shaft (axle).

▼ Using magnetic forces, an electric motor turns electrical energy into moving or kinetic energy.

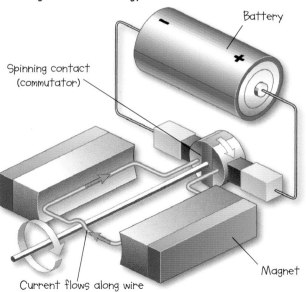

Battery

Spinning contact (commutator)

Current flows along wire

Magnet

18 Engines that burn fuel give out gases and particles through their exhausts. Some of these gases are harmful to the environment. The less we use engines, the better. Electric motors are quiet, efficient and reliable, but they still need fuel – to make the electricity at the power station.

▲ Electric cars have sets of batteries to turn the motor. The batteries are 'filled' with electrical energy by plugging into a recharging point.

QUIZ

1. Are exhaust gases good for the environment?

2. Does a diesel engine use sparks?

3. How many cylinders do most cars have?

4. Do electric cars have batteries?

Answers:
1. No, some of them are harmful
2. No 3. Four or six 4. Yes

Science on the move

19 Without science, you would have to walk everywhere, or ride a horse. Luckily, scientists and engineers have developed many methods of transport, most importantly, the car. Lots of people can travel together in a bus, train, plane or ship. These use less energy and resources, and make less pollution than cars.

▼ Modern airports are enormous. They can stretch for several miles, and they have a constant flow of planes taking off and landing. Hundreds of people are needed to make sure that everything runs smoothly and on time.

Passenger terminal

Jetway

20 Science is used to stop criminals. Science-based security measures include a 'door frame' that detects metal objects like guns and a scanner that sees inside bags. A sniffer-machine can detect the smell of explosives or illegal drugs.

QUIZ

1. How do air traffic controllers talk to pilots?
2. What does a red train signal mean?
3. What powers the supports that move jetways?

Answers:
1. By radio 2. Stop
3. Electric motors

14

21 **Jetways are extending walkways that stretch out from the passenger terminal right to the planes' doors.** Their supports move along on wheeled trolleys driven by electric motors.

22 **Every method of transport needs to be safe and on time.** In the airport control tower, air traffic controllers track planes on radar screens. They talk to pilots by radio. Beacons send out radio signals, giving the direction and distance to the airport.

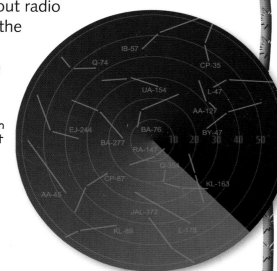

▶ The radar screen shows each aircraft as a blip, with its flight number or identity code.

▼ Train signals show just two colours – red for stop and green for go.

23 **On the road, drivers obey traffic lights.** On a railway network, train drivers obey similar signal lights of different colours, such as red for stop. Sensors by the track record each train passing and send the information by wires or radio to the control room. Each train's position is shown as a flashing light on a wall map.

▶ Trackside switches and detectors react to a train going past and automatically change the signals, so that a following train does not get too close.

Noisy science

24 Listening to the radio or television, playing music, shouting at each other – they all depend on the science of sound – acoustics. Sounds are carried by invisible waves in the air. The waves are areas of low pressure, where air particles are stretched farther apart, alternating with areas of high pressure, where they are squashed closer together.

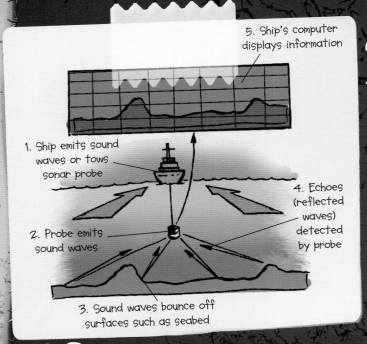

5. Ship's computer displays information

1. Ship emits sound waves or tows sonar probe

2. Probe emits sound waves

3. Sound waves bounce off surfaces such as seabed

4. Echoes (reflected waves) detected by probe

25 Scientists measure the loudness or intensity of sound in decibels, dB. A very quiet sound like a ticking watch is 10 dB. Ordinary speech is 50–60 dB. Loud music is 90 dB. A jet plane taking off is 120 dB. Too much noise damages the ears.

◀ In sonar (echo–sounding), sound waves in the water bounce or reflect off objects, and are detected.

26 Whether a sound is high or low is called its pitch, or frequency. It is measured in Hertz, Hz. A singing bird or whining motorcycle has a high pitch. A rumble of thunder or a massive truck has a low pitch. People can hear frequencies from 25 to 20,000 Hz.

▶ The decibel scale measures the intensity, or energy, in sound.

Atomic explosion

Jet plane

Express train

Whisper

0 dB   40 dB   80 dB   120 dB   180 dB

27

Sound waves spread out from a vibrating object that is moving rapidly to and fro. Stretch an elastic band between your fingers and twang it. As it vibrates, it makes a sound. When you speak, vocal cords in your neck vibrate. You can feel them through your skin.

28

Sound waves travel about 330 metres every second. This is fast, but it is one million times slower than light waves. Sound waves also bounce off hard, flat surfaces. This is called reflection. The returning waves are heard as an echo.

29

Loudspeakers change electrical signals into sounds. The signals in the wire pass through a wire coil inside the speaker. This turns the coil into a magnet, which pushes and pulls against another magnet. The pushing and pulling make the cone vibrate, which sends sound waves into the air.

◀ The word 'sonic' means making sounds, and the high-pitched noises of bats can be described as 'ultrasonic' – too high for us to hear.

Echoes bouncing back off the moth

Sound waves from the bat

▲ Bats make high-pitched sounds. If the sounds hit an insect they bounce back to the bat's ears. The reflected sound (echo) gives the bat information about the size and location of the insect.

BOX GUITAR

You will need:
shoebox   elastic band
split pins   card

Cut a hole about 10 centimetres across on one side of an empty shoebox. Push split pins through either side of the hole, and stretch an elastic band between them. Pluck the band. Hear how the air and box vibrate. Cover the hole with card. Is the 'guitar' as loud?

Look out – light's about!

30 Almost everything you do depends on light and the science of light, which is called optics. Light is a form of energy that you can see. Light waves are made of electricity and magnetism – and they are tiny. About 2000 of them laid end to end would stretch across this full stop.

▶ A prism of clear glass or clear plastic separates the colours in white light.

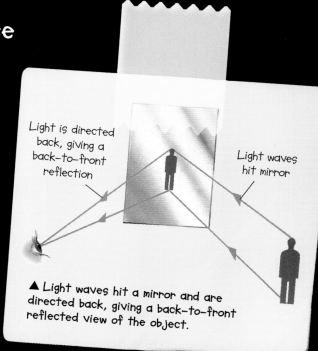

Light is directed back, giving a back–to–front reflection

Light waves hit mirror

▲ Light waves hit a mirror and are directed back, giving a back–to–front reflected view of the object.

32 Like sound, light bounces off surfaces that are very smooth. This is called reflection. A mirror is smooth, hard and flat. When you look at it, you see your reflection.

31 Ordinary light from the Sun or from a light bulb is called white light. But when white light passes through a prism, a triangular block of clear glass, it splits into many colours. These colours are known as the spectrum. Each colour has a different length of wave. A rainbow is made by raindrops, which work like millions of tiny prisms to split up sunlight.

33 Light passes through certain materials, like clear glass and plastic. Materials that let light pass through, to give a clear view, are transparent. Those that do not allow light through, like wood and metal, are opaque.

34 Mirrors and lenses are important parts of many optical (light-using) gadgets. They are found in cameras, binoculars, microscopes, telescopes and lasers. Without them, we would have no close-up photographs of tiny microchips or insects or giant planets – in fact, no photos at all.

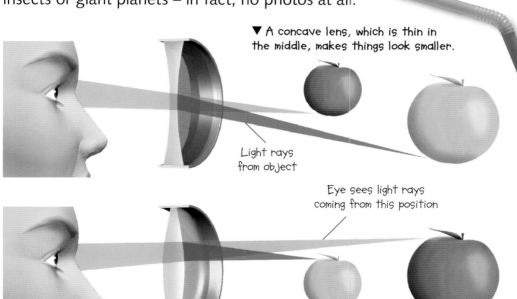

▼ A concave lens, which is thin in the middle, makes things look smaller.

Light rays from object

Eye sees light rays coming from this position

▲ A convex lens, which bulges in the middle, makes things look larger.

35 Light does not usually go straight through glass. It bends slightly where it goes into the glass, then bends back as it comes out. This is called refraction. A lens is a curved piece of glass or plastic that bends light to make things look bigger, smaller or clearer. Spectacle and contact lenses bend light to help people see more clearly.

▲ Glass and water bend, or refract, light waves. This makes a drinking straw look bent where it goes behind the glass and then into the water.

The power of lasers

36 Laser light is a special kind of light. Like ordinary light, it is made of waves, but it has three main differences. Ordinary white light is a mixture of colours, while laser light is one pure colour. Ordinary light waves have peaks (highs) and troughs (lows), which do not line up – laser light waves line up perfectly. Lastly, ordinary light spreads and fades. A laser beam can travel for thousands of kilometres as a strong, straight beam.

◀ The narrow horizontal beam from a laser spirit level can shine all the way across a building site.

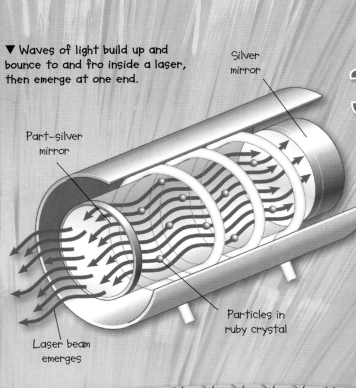

▼ Waves of light build up and bounce to and fro inside a laser, then emerge at one end.

Silver mirror

Part-silver mirror

Particles in ruby crystal

Laser beam emerges

37 To make a laser beam, energy is fed in short bursts into a substance called the active medium. The energy might be electricity, heat or ordinary light. In a red ruby laser, the active medium is a rod of ruby crystal. A strong lamp makes the particles in the crystal vibrate. The energy they give off bounces to and fro inside the crystal. Eventually, the rays vibrate with each other and they are all the same length. The energy becomes so strong that it bursts through a mirror at one end of the crystal.

Beam bounces
off CD

Laser

Spinning CD

Laser beam
bent by prism

Reflected
beam passes
through prism

Reflected beam
detected by sensor

▲ A CD laser
detects tiny pits in
the disc's underside.

▲ In a spectacular outdoor light show,
different coloured laser beams sweep to
and fro as they pierce the darkness,
seemingly all the way into space.

38 Lasers were invented in 1960.
They are used to play CDs and DVDs for
music and movies, and in computers. They cut
through thick metal in factories, and carry out
delicate eye operations. They carry phone calls
and television programmes along cables. They
even measure movements of the Earth to
warn of volcanoes or earthquakes.

QUIZ

1. How far can laser beams travel?

2. When were lasers invented?

3. Which everyday machines use lasers?

Answers:
1. Thousands of kilometres
2. 1960 3. DVD players,
CD players, computers

◀ An industrial laser
has the power to melt
metal into gas and cut
a neat line.

Mysterious magnets

39 Without magnets there would be no electric motors, computers or loudspeakers. Magnetism is an invisible force to do with atoms – tiny particles that make up everything. Atoms are made of even smaller particles, including electrons. Magnetism is linked to the way that these line up and move. Most magnetic substances contain iron. As iron makes up a big part of the metallic substance steel, steel is also magnetic.

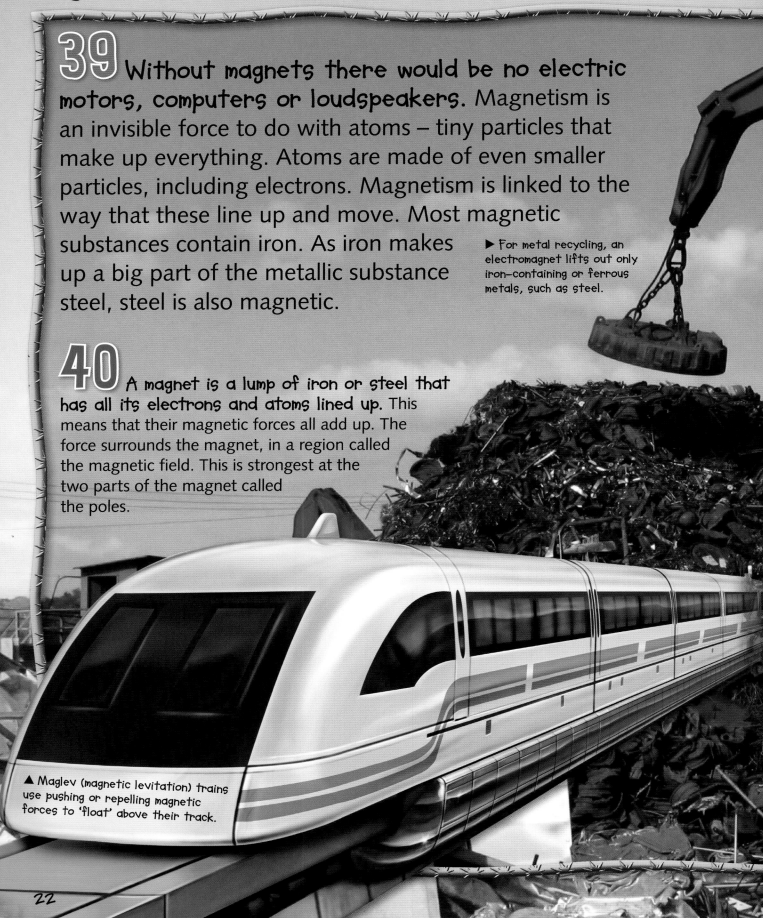

▶ For metal recycling, an electromagnet lifts out only iron-containing or ferrous metals, such as steel.

40 A magnet is a lump of iron or steel that has all its electrons and atoms lined up. This means that their magnetic forces all add up. The force surrounds the magnet, in a region called the magnetic field. This is strongest at the two parts of the magnet called the poles.

▲ Maglev (magnetic levitation) trains use pushing or repelling magnetic forces to 'float' above their track.

41 A magnet has two different poles – north and south. A north pole repels (pushes away) the north pole of another magnet. Two south poles also repel each other. But a north pole and a south pole attract (pull together). Both magnetic poles attract any substance containing iron, like a nail or a screw.

42 When electricity flows through a wire, it makes a weak magnetic field around it. If the wire is wrapped into a coil, the magnetism becomes stronger. This is called an electromagnet. Its magnetic force is the same as an ordinary magnet, but when the electricity goes off, the magnetism does too. Some electromagnets are so strong, they can lift whole cars.

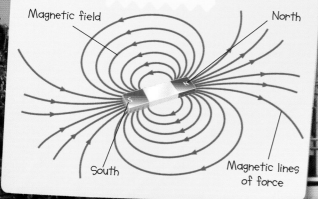

▼ The field around a magnet affects objects that contain iron.

Magnetic field

North

South

Magnetic lines of force

QUIZ

Which of these substances or objects is magnetic?
1. Steel spoon 2. Plastic spoon
3. Pencil 4. Drinks can
5. Food can 6. Screwdriver
7. Cooking foil

Answers:
1. Yes 2. No 3. No
4. No 5. Yes 6. Yes 7. No

Electric sparks!

43 **Flick a switch and things happen.** The television goes off, the computer comes on, lights shine and music plays. Electricity is our favourite form of energy. We send it along wires and plug hundreds of machines into it.

▼ When an electric current flows, the electrons (small blue balls) all move the same way, jumping from one atom to the next. (The red balls are the centres or nuclei of the atoms.)

44 **Electricity depends on electrons.** In certain substances, when electrons are 'pushed', they hop from one atom to the next. When billions do this every second, electricity flows. The 'push' is from a battery or a generator. Electricity only flows in a complete loop or circuit. Break the circuit and the flow stops.

Atom

Electron

▼ Solar panels contain many hundreds of fingernail-sized PV (photovoltaic) cells. These convert light energy ('photo') to electrical energy ('voltaic').

▼ A battery has a chemical paste inside its metal casing.

Positive contact

Negative contact on base

45 **A battery makes electricity from chemicals.** Two different chemicals next to each other, such as an acid and a metal, swap electrons and get the flow going. Electricity's pushing strength is measured in volts. Most batteries are about 1.5, 3, 6 or 9 volts, with 12 volts in cars.

46 **Electricity flows easily through some substances, including water and metals.** These are electrical conductors. Other substances do not allow electricity to flow. They are insulators. Insulators include wood, plastic, glass, card and ceramics. Metal wires and cables have coverings of plastic, to stop the electricity leaking away.

47

Electricity from power stations is carried along cables on high pylons, or buried underground. This is known as the distribution grid. At thousands of volts, this electricity is extremely dangerous. For use in the home, it is changed to 220 volts (in the UK).

▼ Electricity generators are housed in huge casings, some bigger than trucks.

Pylon holds cables off the ground

◄ To check and repair high–voltage cables, the electricity must be turned off well in advance.

48

Mains electricity is made at a power station. A fuel such as coal or oil is burned to heat water into high-pressure steam. The steam pushes past the blades of a turbine and makes them spin. The turbines turn generators, which have wire coils near powerful magnets, and the spinning motion makes electricity flow in the coils.

MAKE A CIRCUIT

You will need:
lightbulb   battery   wire
plastic ruler   metal spoon   dry card

Join a bulb to a battery with pieces of wire, as shown. Electricity flows round the circuit and lights the bulb. Make a gap in the circuit and put various objects into it, to see if they allow electricity to flow again. Try a plastic ruler, a metal spoon and some dry card.

Making sounds and pictures

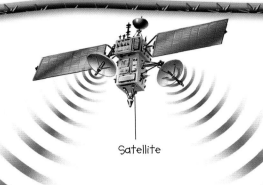

Satellite

Radio waves

49 The air is full of waves we cannot see or hear, unless we have the right machine. Radio waves are a form of electrical and magnetic energy, just like heat and light waves, microwaves and X-rays. All of these are called electromagnetic waves and they travel at an equal speed – the speed of light.

50 Radio waves are used for both radio and television. They travel vast distances. Long waves curve around the Earth's surface. Short waves bounce between the Earth and the sky.

▼ This range of waves, with different wavelengths, are electrical and magnetic energy. They are called the electromagnetic spectrum.

Aerial

▲ A radio set picks up radio waves using its aerial or antenna.

51 Radio waves carry their information by being altered, or modulated, in a certain pattern. The height of a wave is called its amplitude. If this is altered, it is known as AM (amplitude modulation). Look for AM on the radio display.

52 The number of waves per second is called the frequency. If this is altered, it is known as FM (frequency modulation). FM radio is clearer than AM, and less affected by weather and thunderstorms.

| Long radio waves | Shorter radio waves (TV) | Microwaves | Infrared waves | Light waves (visible light) | Ultraviolet rays | X-rays | Short X-rays | Gamma rays |

53 Radio waves are sent out, or transmitted, from antennae on tall masts or on satellites, to reach a very wide area. A radio receiver converts the pattern of waves to sounds. A television receiver or TV set changes them to pictures and sounds.

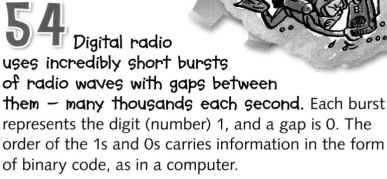

▼ A dish-shaped receiver picks up radio waves for TV channels.

54 Digital radio uses incredibly short bursts of radio waves with gaps between them — many thousands each second. Each burst represents the digit (number) 1, and a gap is 0. The order of the 1s and 0s carries information in the form of binary code, as in a computer.

▶ A plasma screen has thousands of tiny boxes, or cells, of three colours — red, green and blue. Electric pulses heat the gas inside for a split second into plasma, which gives out a burst of light. Combinations of these colours give all the other colours.

▼ Flat-screen TVs can be LCD or plasma. They use less electricity than cathode-ray TVs and produce a better picture.

KEY
1 Glowing 'on' cell
2 Dark 'off' cell
3 Rear grid of electrical contacts
4 – 6 Coloured phosphors inside cells
7 Backing plate
8 Front grid of electrical contacts
9 Transparent front cover

Compu-science

55 **Computers are amazing machines, but they have to be told exactly what to do.** So we put in instructions and information, by various means. These include typing on a keyboard, inserting a disc or memory stick, downloading from the Internet, using a joystick or games controller, or linking up a camera, scanner or another computer.

56 **Most computers are controlled by instructions from a keyboard and a mouse.** The mouse moves a pointer around on the screen and its click buttons select choices from lists called menus.

Silicon 'wafer'

Plastic casing

Wire 'feet' link to other parts in the computer

◀ This close up of a slice of silicon 'wafer' shows the tiny parts that receive and send information in a computer.

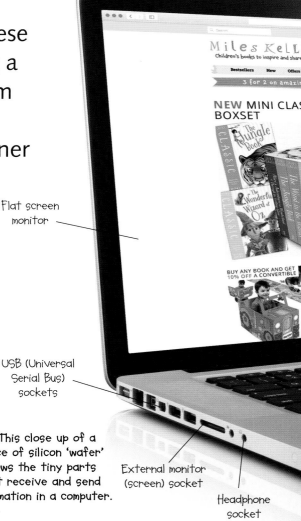

Flat screen monitor

USB (Universal Serial Bus) sockets

External monitor (screen) socket

Headphone socket

57 **Some computers are controlled by talking to them!** They pick up the sounds using a microphone. This is speech recognition technology.

58 **The 'main brain' of a computer is its Central Processing Unit.** It is usually a microchip – millions of electronic parts on a chip of silicon, hardly larger than a fingernail. It receives information and instructions from other microchips, carries out the work, and sends back the results.

QUIZ

You may have heard of these sets of letters. Do you know what they mean? Their full written-out versions are all here on these two pages.

1. RAM 2. ROM
3. CPU

Answers:
1. Random Access Memory
2. Read Only Memory
3. Central Processing Unit

▲ Launched in 2010, the Apple iPad began a new trend in computerized devices called 'tablets'.

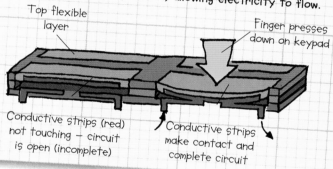

▼ The keys on a keyboard have bendy metal contacts that come together when pressed, allowing electricity to flow.

Top flexible layer

Finger presses down on keypad

Conductive strips (red) not touching – circuit is open (incomplete)

Conductive strips make contact and complete circuit

CD or DVD drive reader

Mouse pad

Keyboard

▲ As well as desktop computers, there are also laptops with a fold-up LCD (liquid crystal display) screen. Touching the mouse pad with a finger controls the cursor or insert point on the screen.

59 Information and instructions are contained in the computer in memory microchips. There are two kinds. Random Access Memory is like a jotting pad. It keeps changing as the computer carries out its tasks. Read Only Memory is like an instruction book. It usually contains the instructions for how the computer starts up and how all the microchips work together.

60 A computer usually displays its progress on a monitor screen. It feeds information to output devices such as printers, loudspeakers and robot arms. Information can be stored on CDs, DVDs, memory sticks (chips), external HDs (hard drive discs), or uploaded to the Internet.

Web around the world

61 The world is at your fingertips — if you are on the Internet. The Internet is one of the most amazing results of science. It is a worldwide network of computers, linked like one huge electrical spider's web.

62 Signals travel between computers in many ways. These include electricity along telephone wires, flashes of laser light along fibre-optic cables or radio waves between tall towers. Information is changed from one form to another in a split second. It can also travel between computers on different sides of the world in less than a second using satellite links.

First 'private' Internet, ARPANET, for the US military

Joint Academic Network (JANET) connects UK universities via their own Internet

Yahoo! Launches as a 'Guide to the World Wide Web' — what we now call a browser or search engine

Animation starts to become common on websites

1969　　**1984**　　**1994**　　**1996**

1961　　**1972**　　**1989**　　**1995**

First ideas for 'packet switching', the basic way the Internet parcels up and sends information in small blocks or packets

First emails, mostly on ARPANET

The birth of the Internet as we know it today, when Tim Berners-Lee and the team at CERN invent the World Wide Web to make information easier to publish and access

eBay and Amazon booksellers begin, and online trade starts to rise

63 The World Wide Web is public information that anyone can find on the Internet, available for everyone to see. However, sometimes you have to pay or join a club to get to certain parts of it. A website is a collection of related information, usually made up of text, videos and pictures. There might be hundreds of web pages within each website. Email is the system for sending private messages from one person to another.

I DON'T BELIEVE IT!

The World Wide Web is the best known and most widely used part of the Internet system. It has billions of pages of information.

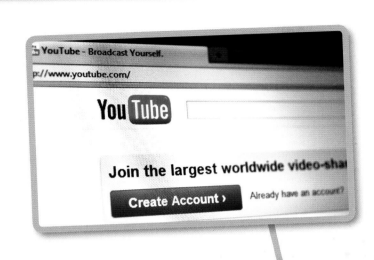

▼ Many mobile phones can be used to access the Internet, allowing users to browse web pages, send emails, watch videos, and use apps such as Instagram and WhatsApp.

Half of households in the UK have Internet connections

YouTube is launched, allowing video sharing

The first iPhones bring mobile Internet use for almost anyone

Facebook has fewer new users signing up — is the slower growth temporary, or the beginning of the end for online social networking?

2003   **2005**   **2007**   **2011**

1998   **2004**   **2006**   **2010**

Google is launched as a rival to Yahoo!

Facebook is launched, starting the trend for social networking over the Internet

Twitter is launched for posting and sharing text messages, but has a slow start

HD (High Definition) Internet video links become more practical

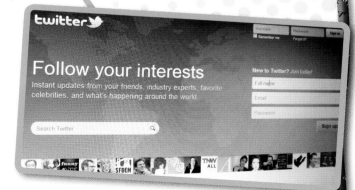

▲ The Web and the Internet interact with other technologies. Twitter is an online public version of text-only messages called 'tweets' developed from mobile phone 'texting' (SMS, Short Message Service).

31

What's it made of?

64 You wouldn't make a bridge out of straw, or a cup out of bubblewrap. Choosing the right substance for the job is important. All the substances in the world can be divided into several groups. For example, metals such as iron, silver and gold are strong, hard and shiny, and conduct heat and electricity well. They are used to make things that have to be strong and long-lasting.

65 Plastics are made mainly from the substances in petroleum (crude oil). There are so many kinds – some are hard and brittle while others are soft and bendy. They are usually long-lasting, not affected by weather or damp, and they resist heat and electricity.

KEY

① The front wing is a special shape – this produces a force that presses the car down onto the track

② The main body of the car is made from carbon fibre, a light but very strong material

③ The car's axles are made from titanium – a very strong, light metal

④ The engine is made from various alloys, or mixtures of metals, based on aluminium. It produces up to ten times the power of a family car engine

⑤ Each tyre is made of thick, tough rubber to withstand high speeds

⑥ The rear wing is also carbon fibre composite

▼ A racing car has thousands of parts made from hundreds of materials. Each is suited to certain conditions such as stress, temperature and vibrations.

66 Ceramics are materials based on clay or other substances dug from the Earth. They can be shaped and dried, like a clay bowl. Or they can be fired – baked in a hot oven called a kiln. This makes them hard and long-lasting, but brittle and prone to cracks. Ceramics resist heat and electricity very well.

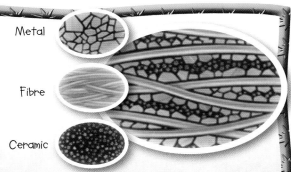

Metal

Fibre

Ceramic

▲ Metal, fibre and ceramic can combine to make a composite material. The way all of these ingredients are arranged can affect the composite's strength.

◄ In 2007, the Interstate 35W bridge collapsed in Minneapolis, USA, killing 13 people. It was due to cracking of small steel connecting plates that were too thin for the weight.

67 Glass is produced from the raw substances limestone and sand. When heated at a high temperature, these substances become a clear, gooey liquid, which sets hard as it cools. Its great advantage is that you can see through it.

68 Composites are mixtures or combinations of different materials. For example, glass strands are coated with plastic to make GRP – glass-reinforced plastic. This composite has the advantages of both materials.

MAKE YOUR OWN COMPOSITE

You will need:
flour   newspaper strips
water   balloon   pin

You can make a composite called pâpier maché from flour, newspaper and water. Tear newspaper into strips. Mix flour and water into a paste. Dip each strip in the paste and place it around a blown-up balloon. Cover the balloon and allow it to dry. Pop the balloon with a pin, and the composite should stay in shape.

World of chemicals

69 The world is made of chemical substances. Some are completely pure. Others are mixtures of substances – such as petroleum (crude oil). Petroleum provides us with thousands of different chemicals and materials, such as plastics, paints, soaps and fuels. It is one of the most useful, and valuable, substances in the world.

Fuel gases for burning

The fumes cool as they rise up the tower, causing them to condense

Petrol and vehicle fuels

Kerosene and medium fuels (jet fuel)

Heavy oils for lubrication

Furnace

Waxes, tars, bitumens, asphalts

Crude oil is super-heated and some parts turn into fumes

▼ The biggest offshore oil platforms are more than 150 metres tall above the ocean surface. They drill boreholes into the seabed and pump up the crude oil, or petroleum.

▲ The huge tower (fractionating column) of an oil refinery may be 100 metres high.

70 In an oil refinery, crude oil is heated in a huge tower. Some of its different substances turn into fumes and rise up the tower. The fumes condense (turn back into liquids) at different heights inside, due to the different temperatures at each level. Thick, gooey tars, asphalts and bitumens – used to make road surfaces – remain at the bottom.

71 One group of chemicals is called acids. They vary in strength from very weak citric acid, which gives the sharp taste to fruits such as lemons, to extremely strong and dangerous sulphuric acid in a car battery. Powerful acids burn and corrode, or eat away, substances. Some even corrode glass or steel.

72 Another group of chemicals is bases. They vary in strength from weak alkaloids, which give the bitter taste to coffee beans, to strong and dangerous bases in drain cleaners and industrial polishes. Bases feel soapy or slimy and, like acids, they can burn or corrode.

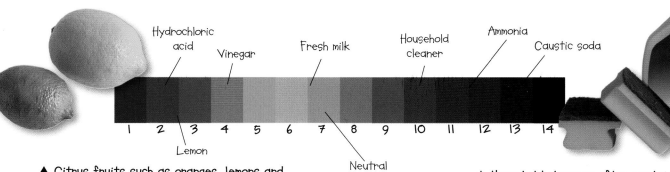

Hydrochloric acid · Vinegar · Fresh milk · Household cleaner · Ammonia · Caustic soda

1 2 3 4 5 6 7 8 9 10 11 12 13 14

Lemon

Neutral

▲ Citrus fruits such as oranges, lemons and limes have a tart taste because they contain a mild acid, called citric acid. It has a pH (potential of hydrogen) of 3. pH is the scale of acidity.

▲ Household cleaners often contain alkalis to help them break down grease and fat. Some cleaners have a pH of 10.

Acidic substance

Neutral substance

Alkaline substance

► Indicator paper changes colour when it touches different substances. Acids turn it red, alkalis make it bluish-purple. The deeper the colour, the stronger the acid or base.

73 Acids and bases are 'opposite' types of chemicals. When they meet, they undergo changes called a chemical reaction. The result is usually a third type of chemical, called a salt. The common salt we use for cooking is one example. Its chemical name is sodium chloride.

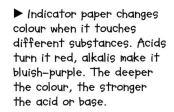

FROTHY FUN

You will need:
vinegar   washing soda
Create a chemical reaction by adding a few drops of vinegar to a spoonful of washing soda in a saucer. The vinegar is an acid, the soda is a base. The two react by frothing and giving off bubbles of carbon dioxide gas. What is left is a salt (but not to be eaten).

Pure science

74 The world seems to be made of millions of different substances — such as soil, wood, concrete, plastics and air. These are combinations of simpler substances. If you could take them apart, you would see that they are made of pure substances called elements.

1	2	3	4	5	6	7	8	9	10	11	12
1 H Hydrogen											
3 Li Lithium	4 Be Beryllium										
11 Na Sodium	12 Mg Magnesium										
19 K Potassium	20 Ca Calcium	21 Sc Scandium	22 Ti Titanium	23 V Vanadium	24 Cr Chromium	25 Mn Manganese	26 Fe Iron	27 Co Colbalt	28 Ni Nickel	29 Cu Copper	30 Zn Zinc
37 Rb Rubidium	38 Sr Strontium	39 Y Yttrium	40 Zr Zirconium	41 Nb Niobium	42 Mo Molybdenum	43 Tc Technetium	44 Ru Ruthenium	45 Rh Rhodium	46 Pd Palladium	47 Ag Silver	48 Cd Cadmium
55 Cs Caesium	56 Ba Barium	Elements 57–71	72 Hf Hafnium	73 Ta Tantalum	74 W Tungsten	75 Re Rhenium	76 Os Osmium	77 Ir Iridium	78 Pt Platinum	79 Au Gold	80 Hg Mercury
87 Fr Francium	88 Ra Radium	Elements 89–103	104 Rf Rutherfordium	105 Db Dubnium	106 Sg Seaborgium	107 Bh Bohrium	108 HS Hassium	109 Mt Meitnerium	110 Ds Darmstadtium	111 Rg Roentgenium	112 Uub Ununbium

Atomic number / Chemical symbol / Name

20 Ca Calcium

57 La Lanthanum	58 Ce Cerium	59 Pr Praseodymium	60 Nd Neodymium	61 Pm Promethium	62 Sm Samarium	63 Eu Europium	64 Gd Gadolinium	65 Tb Terbium
89 Ac Actinium	90 Th Thorium	91 Pa Protactinium	92 U Uranium	93 Np Neptunium	94 Pu Plutonium	95 Am Americium	96 Cm Curium	97 Bk Berkelium

▶ Stars are made mainly of burning hydrogen, which is why they are so hot and bright.

▲ The Periodic Table is a chart of all the elements. In each row the atoms get heavier from left to right. Each column (up–down) contains elements with similar chemical features. Every element has a chemical symbol, name, and atomic number, which is the number of particles called protons in its central part, or nucleus. The Periodic Table can be updated with new elements.

75 Hydrogen is the simplest element and it is the first in the Periodic Table. This means it has the smallest atoms. It is a very light gas, which floats upwards in air. Hydrogen was used to fill giant airships. But there was a problem — hydrogen catches fire easily and explodes.

76 About 90 elements are found naturally on and in the Earth. In an element, all of its particles, called atoms, are exactly the same as each other. Just as important, they are all different from the atoms of any other element.

Element types
- ■ Alkali metals
- ■ Alkaline metals
- ■ Transition metals
- ■ Other metals
- ■ Other non-metals
- ■ Halogens
- ■ Inert gases
- ■ Lanthanides
- ■ Actinides
- ■ Trans-actinides

Note: Elements 113–118 are synthetic elements that have only been created briefly, so their properties cannot be known for certain.

					18
					2 He Helium
13	**14**	**15**	**16**	**17**	
5 B Boron	6 C Carbon	7 N Nitrogen	8 O Oxygen	9 F Fluorine	10 Ne Neon
13 Al Aluminium	14 Si Silicon	15 P Phosphorus	16 S Sulphur	17 Cl Chlorine	18 Ar Argon
31 Ga Gallium	32 Ge Germanium	33 As Arsenic	34 Se Selenium	35 Br Bromine	36 Kr Krypton
49 In Indium	50 Sn Tin	51 Sb Antimony	52 Te Tellurium	53 I Iodine	54 Xe Xenon
81 Ti Thallium	82 Pb Lead	83 Bi Bismuth	84 Po Polonium	85 At Astatine	86 Rn Radon
113 Nh Nihonium	114 Fl Flerovium	115 Mc Moscovium	116 Lv Livermorium	117 Ts Tennessine	118 Og Oganesson

66 Dy Dysprosium	67 Ho Holmium	68 Er Erbium	69 Tm Thulium	70 Yb Ytterbium	71 Lu Lutetium
98 Cf Californium	99 Es Einsteinium	100 Fm Fermium	101 Md Mendelevium	102 No Nobelium	103 Lr Lawrencium

QUIZ

1. How many elements are found naturally on Earth?
2. Which lightweight metal is very useful?
3. Which element makes up stars?
4. What do diamonds and coal have in common?

Answers:
1. About 90 2. Aluminium 3. Hydrogen 4. They are both made of pure carbon

78 Uranium is a heavy and dangerous element. It gives off harmful rays and tiny particles. This process is called radioactivity and it can cause sickness, burns and diseases such as cancer. Radioactivity is a form of energy and, under careful control, radioactive elements are used as fuel in nuclear power stations.

▶ Aluminium is a strong but light metal that is ideal for forming the body of vehicles such as planes.

77 Carbon is a very important element in living things – including our own bodies. It joins easily with atoms of other elements to make large groups of atoms called molecules. When it is pure, carbon can be two different forms. These are soft, powdery soot, and hard, glittering diamond. The form depends on how the carbon atoms join to each other.

79 Aluminium is an element that is a metal, and it is one of the most useful in modern life. It is light and strong, it does not rust, and it is resistant to corrosion. Saucepans, drinks cans, cooking foil and jet planes are made mainly of aluminium.

Bond (link)   Atom

◀ Diamond is a form of the element carbon where the atoms are linked, or bonded, in a very strong box-like pattern.

80 Many pages in this book mention atoms. They are the smallest bits of a substance. They are so tiny, even a billion atoms would be too small to see. But scientists have carried out experiments to find out what's inside an atom. The answer is – even smaller bits. These are sub-atomic particles, and there are three main kinds.

81 At the centre of each atom is a blob called the nucleus. It contains two kinds of sub-atomic particles. These are protons and neutrons. Protons are positive, or plus. The neutron is neither positive nor negative. Around the centre of each atom are sub–atomic particles called electrons. They whizz round the nucleus. In the same way that a proton in the nucleus is positive or plus, an electron negative or minus. The number of protons and electrons is usually the same.

82 Atoms of the various elements have different numbers of protons and neutrons. An atom of hydrogen has just one proton. An atom of helium, the gas put in party balloons to make them float, has two protons and two neutrons. An atom of the heavy metal called lead has 82 protons and 124 neutrons.

I DON'T BELIEVE IT!

One hundred years ago, people thought the electrons were spread out in an atom, like the raisins in a raisin pudding.

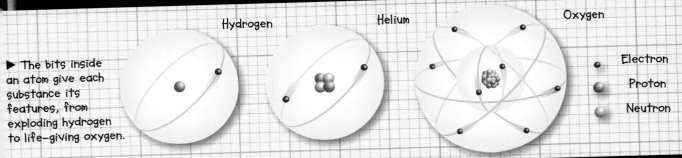

Hydrogen   Helium   Oxygen

▶ The bits inside an atom give each substance its features, from exploding hydrogen to life–giving oxygen.

Electron

Proton

Neutron

83 **It is hard to imagine the size of an atom.** A grain of sand, smaller than this o, contains at least 100 billion billion atoms. If you could make the atoms bigger, so that each one becomes as big as a pin head, the grain of sand would be 2 kilometres high!

Electron

Nucleus made from protons and neutrons

Movement of electrons

▲ The protons and neutrons in the nucleus of an atom are held together by a powerful force.

84 **'Nano' means one–billionth (1/1,000,000,000th), and nanotechnology is science at the smallest level — how atoms join to make molecules.** It is fairly new, but it has already produced many useful products, from stronger materials in jet planes and racing cars, to self-cleaning glass and bouncier tennis balls!

◀ This idea for a nano gear–bearing allows the central axle to spin inside the outer collar. It could be used in micromachines.

▼ Buckyballs are ball–shaped structures made of carbon atoms, used in some types of solar panels and medical research.

▶ Like buckyballs, nanotubes are formed mainly of carbon atoms. They can be combined with plastics in hi–tech equipment such as racing bicycles.

Scientists at work

85 There are thousands of different jobs and careers in science. Scientists work in laboratories, factories, offices, mines, steelworks, nature parks and almost everywhere else. They find new knowledge and make discoveries using a process called the scientific method.

86 First comes an idea, called a theory or hypothesis. This asks or predicts what will happen in a certain situation. Scientists continually come up with new ideas and theories to test. One very simple theory is – if I throw a ball up in the air, will it come back down?

▲ Some scientific work involves handling microbes or dangerous chemicals. This means safety precautions such as wearing gloves and a face mask may be necessary.

▶ In scientific terms, throwing a ball into the air is an experiment. What will be the result?

QUIZ
Put these activities in the correct order, so that a scientist can carry out the scientific method.
1. Results 2. Experiment
3. Conclusions 4. Theory
5. Measurements

Answer:
4, 2, 5, 1, 3

87 The scientist carries out an experiment or test, to check what happens. The experiment is carefully designed and controlled, so that it will reveal useful results. Any changes are carried out one at a time, so that the effect of each change can be studied. The experiment for our simple theory is – throw the ball up in the air.

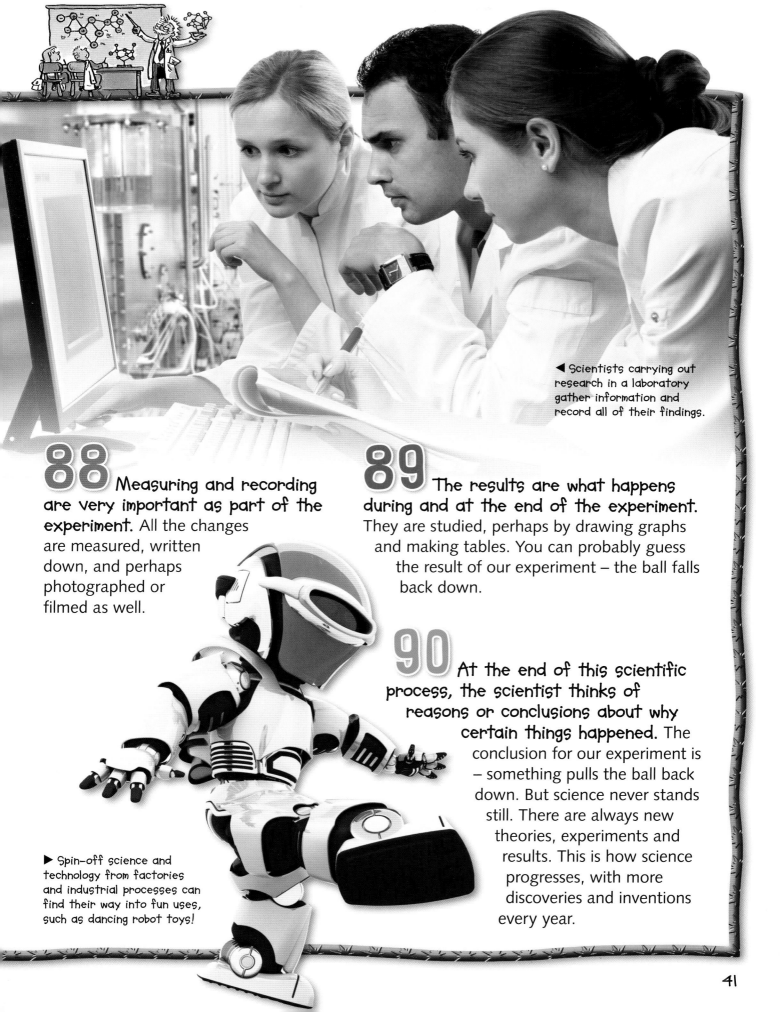

◀ Scientists carrying out research in a laboratory gather information and record all of their findings.

88 Measuring and recording are very important as part of the experiment. All the changes are measured, written down, and perhaps photographed or filmed as well.

89 The results are what happens during and at the end of the experiment. They are studied, perhaps by drawing graphs and making tables. You can probably guess the result of our experiment – the ball falls back down.

90 At the end of this scientific process, the scientist thinks of reasons or conclusions about why certain things happened. The conclusion for our experiment is – something pulls the ball back down. But science never stands still. There are always new theories, experiments and results. This is how science progresses, with more discoveries and inventions every year.

▶ Spin-off science and technology from factories and industrial processes can find their way into fun uses, such as dancing robot toys!

Science in nature

91 Science and its effects are found all over the natural world. Scientists study animals, plants, rocks and soil. They want to understand nature, and find out how science and its technology affect wildlife.

▼ One of the most important jobs in science is to study damage and pollution in the natural world. Almost everything we do affects wild places and animals and plants. For example, the power station here may make the river water warmer. This could encourage animals and plants accidentally introduced from tropical areas, which change the balance of nature.

92 One of the most complicated types of science is ecology. Ecologists try to understand how the natural world links together. They study how animals and plants live, what animals eat, and why plants grow better in some soils than others. They count the numbers of animals and plants and may trap animals briefly to study them, or follow the growth of trees in a wood. When the balance of nature is damaged, ecologists can help to find out why.

▼ The science of ecology involves long periods of studying nature in all kinds of habitats, from rivers to the seabed. For example, observing birds like herons, and fish such as trout, shows which foods they eat. This helps us to understand how changes to the habitat may affect them.

KEY
1. Water beetle
2. Rainbow trout
3. Water scorpion
4. Banded demoiselle damselfly
5. Heron
6. Otter
7. Warbler
8. Power station
9. Reedmace

I DON'T BELIEVE IT!

Science explains how animals such as birds or whales find their way across the world. Some detect the Earth's magnetism, and which way is north or south. Others follow changes in gravity, the force that pulls everything to the Earth's surface.

◄ Oil spills and leaks cause vast damage to a region's ecology. Scientists advise on the best ways to clear up the pollution.

93 Ecologists use many forms of high-tech science in their studies. They may fit an animal with a radio-collar so that its movements can be tracked. Special cameras see in the dark and show how night hunters catch their prey. Radar used to detect planes can also follow flocks of birds. The sonar (echo-sounding) equipment of boats can track shoals of fish or whales.

◄ Tracking tigers is vital to know the threats faced by these endangered big cats, and help to save them.

Body science

94 One of the biggest areas of science is medicine. Medical scientists work to produce better drugs, more spare parts for the body and more machines for use by doctors. They also carry out scientific research to find out how people can stay healthy and prevent disease.

▲ Medical technology uses the latest equipment to diagnose illness, treat life-threatening conditions and cure diseases. This monitoring unit displays heart rate, pulse rate, amounts of oxygen in the blood, breathing speed, blood pressure and other vital signs.

95

As parts of the body work, such as the muscles and nerves, they produce tiny pulses of electricity. Pads on the skin pick up these pulses, which are displayed as a wavy line on a screen or paper strip. The ECG (electro-cardiograph) machine shows the heart beating. The EEG (electro-encephalograph) shows nerve signals flashing around the brain.

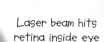
Laser beam hits retina inside eye

▶ A laser beam shines safely through the front of the eye to mend inner problems such as a detached retina.

MAKE A PULSE MACHINE

You will need:
modelling clay   drinking straw

Find your pulse by feeling your wrist, just below the base of your thumb, with a finger of the other hand. Place some modelling clay on this area, and stick a drinking straw into it. Watch the straw twitch with each heartbeat. Now you can see and feel your pulse. Check your pulse rate by counting the number of heartbeats in one minute.

96

Laser beams are ideal for delicate operations, or surgery, on body parts such as the eye. The beam makes very small, precise cuts. It can be shone into the eye and made more focused, or strongest, inside. So it can make a cut deep within the eye, without any harm to the outer parts.

▶ An endoscope is inserted into the body to give a doctor a picture on screen. The treatment can be given immediately.

97

The endoscope is like a flexible telescope made of fibre-strands. This is pushed into a body opening such as the mouth, or through a small cut, to see inside. The surgeon looks into the other end of the endoscope, or at a picture on a screen.

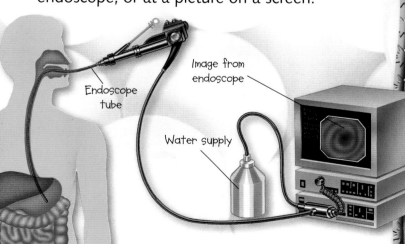
Endoscope tube
Image from endoscope
Water supply

Science in the future

98 Many modern machines and processes can cause damage to our environment and our health. The damage includes acid rain, destruction of the ozone layer and the greenhouse effect, leading to climate change and global warming. Science can help to find solutions. New filters and chemicals called catalysts can reduce dangerous fumes from vehicle exhausts and power stations, and in the chemicals in factory waste pipes.

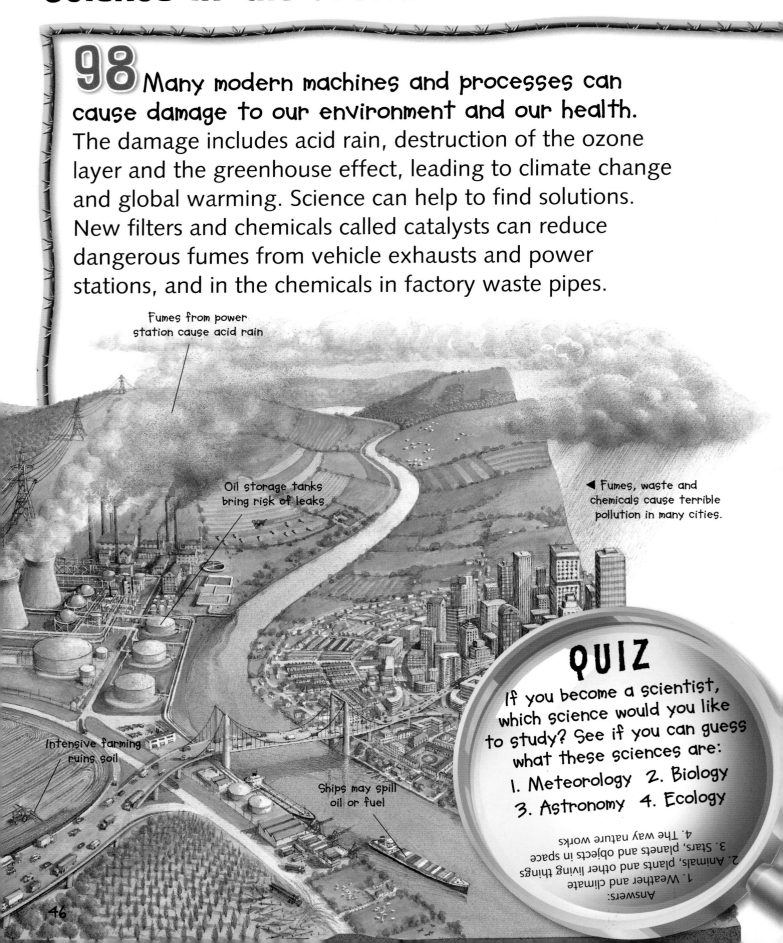

Fumes from power station cause acid rain

Oil storage tanks bring risk of leaks

◄ Fumes, waste and chemicals cause terrible pollution in many cities.

Intensive farming ruins soil

Ships may spill oil or fuel

QUIZ

If you become a scientist, which science would you like to study? See if you can guess what these sciences are:

1. Meteorology 2. Biology
3. Astronomy 4. Ecology

Answers:
1. Weather and climate
2. Animals, plants and other living things
3. Stars, planets and objects in space
4. The way nature works

Bottles crushed

Crushed glass into furnace

Bottle bank for empty glassware

Molten glass poured into moulds

Bottles cool and glass hardens

Bottles filled and used

▶ Sorting waste into different materials such as glass, plastic and cardboard before it is collected makes recycling much more efficient.

▲ Recycling glass saves enormous amounts of energy and raw materials.

99 One very important area of science is recycling. Many materials and substances can be recycled – glass, paper, plastics, cans, scrap metals and rags. Scientists are working to improve the process. Products should be designed so that when they no longer work, they are easy to recycle. The recycling process itself is also being made more effective.

100 We use vast amounts of energy, especially to make electricity and as fuel in our cars. Much of this energy comes from crude oil (petroleum), natural gas and coal. But these energy sources will not last for ever. They also cause huge amounts of pollution. Scientists are working to develop cleaner forms of energy, which will produce less pollution and not run out. These include wind power from turbines, solar power from photocells, and hydroelectric and tidal power from dams.

Rotor blade

Spinner

Pylon

▶ In a wind turbine, the mechanical spinning movement from the rotor is changed into electrical energy.

GREAT SCIENTISTS

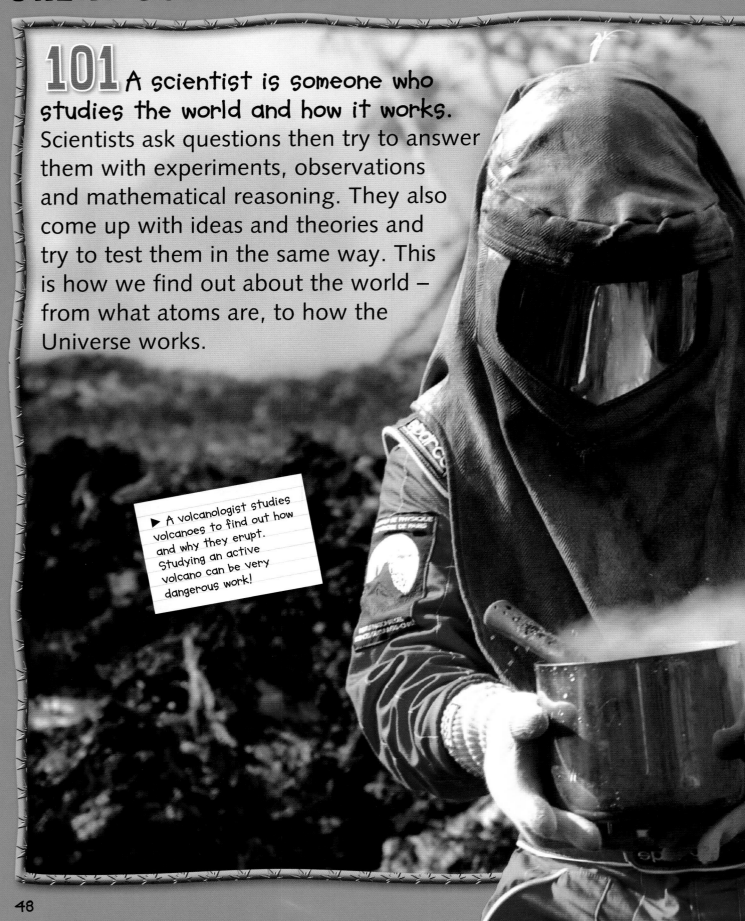

101 A scientist is someone who studies the world and how it works. Scientists ask questions then try to answer them with experiments, observations and mathematical reasoning. They also come up with ideas and theories and try to test them in the same way. This is how we find out about the world – from what atoms are, to how the Universe works.

▶ A volcanologist studies volcanoes to find out how and why they erupt. Studying an active volcano can be very dangerous work!

102

Scientific ideas are constantly changing. What scientists think is true in one age may be questioned in the next. Just a century ago, astronomers thought the Universe was no bigger than our Milky Way Galaxy. We now know the Universe is much vaster, with more than 500 billion galaxies.

▶ There are many different kinds of scientist. They specialize in different fields, such as particle physicists who study atoms and microbiologists who study microscopic life.

103

In the past, scientists often studied a wide range of subjects. In fact, the word 'scientist' was not widely used until 1830. Most of the great scientists in this book from before that time were called 'natural philosophers'.

Life sciences

Botany...............	Botanists study plants in nature and the laboratory
Zoology..............	Zoologists study animals in nature and the laboratory
Genetics.............	Genetics is the science of how living things pass on features to offspring
Medicine.............	Medicine is the science of understanding and healing the human body

Physical Sciences

Physics...............	Physicists study matter and forces and how they move through space and time
Chemistry............	Chemists study substances and how they react with each other
Astronomy...........	Astronomers study space – from moons and planets to stars and galaxies

Earth Sciences

Geology..............	Geologists study rocks and minerals and how the Earth works
Oceanography........	Oceanographers study the oceans and ocean currents and tides
Palaeontology......	Palaeontologists study prehistoric life and fossils
Meteorology........	Meteorologists study the weather, climate and changes in the atmosphere

Mathematical marvels

104 About 10,000 years ago, people in the Middle East began to farm. They built great civilizations, such as ancient Egypt, and developed numbers, which helped to keep a record of things. They discovered that numbers could be used to work things out, such as fair shares or the area of a field. This is how mathematics began.

▼ The ancient Egyptians built the pyramids with amazing accuracy. They could work out the height of a pyramid just from the length of its shadow.

Euclid
Greek c.300 BC

◄ The Shard in London is a brand new building that was completed in 2012. Modern engineers have based their ideas on Euclid's ancient proof.

105 In ancient Greece, mathematicians worked out things such as the areas of triangles. They set out logical proof of their ideas. The greatest mathematician was Euclid, whose book 'Elements' still provides basic skills used by engineers and builders today.

Archimedes
Greek 287–212 BC

106 Archimedes thought about problems in a scientific way. He came up with theories that could be proved or disproved by experiments and mathematics. Archimedes proved that the power of a lever (a simple machine) to move a load depends on how far from its pivot point (point of rotation) you apply your effort.

107

A story tells how the king of Syracuse suspected impure gold had been used to make his crown. Archimedes was asked to investigate. But how could he tell without melting the crown? He hit on the solution while in his bath, and was so excited he ran naked through the streets shouting, 'Eureka!' (which means, 'I've got it!').

108

Archimedes explained how things float. When an object sinks down in water, the water pushes it back up with a force equal to the weight of water displaced (pushed away). The object has a natural upthrust or 'buoyancy'. He showed that an object sinks until its weight is equal to the weight of water displaced, then it floats.

◀▼ Heavy ships float because they are supported by the weight of water they push out of the way.

The weight of the ship is equal to the water it displaces

When the ship sinks down, the water it displaces thrusts it back up with equal force

109

Archimedes launched a giant ship on his own using levers and pulleys. A pulley turns around like a wheel and has a groove for a cable or rope. Lots of pulleys allow us to lift heavy weights easily.

▼ Archimedes identified three types (classes) of lever, according to where you apply effort in relation to the pivot.

① A **class 1** lever has the load and effort on opposite sides of the pivot or fulcrum, like a seesaw

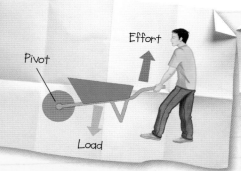

② A **class 2** lever has the load and effort on the same side of the pivot, as in a wheelbarrow

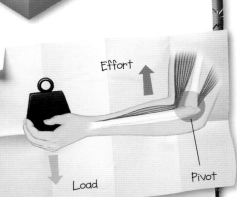

③ A **class 3** lever has the effort between the load and the pivot, like a human elbow

Baghdad brilliance

Ibn Sina Avicenna
Persian c.980–1037

110 When Muhammad began to teach the religion of Islam in the 600s, he charged followers to search for knowledge. Baghdad and other Islamic cities became centres of learning. Ibn Sina studied everything from philosophy to physics. He not only identified the main forms of energy and the idea of force, he wrote a book, *The Canon of Medicine*, which became the doctors' bible for 600 years.

QUIZ

1. What did the astrolabe measure?
2. What is distillation used for today?
3. What does algebra use to replace unknown numbers in calculations?

Answers:
1. Angles 2. For refining oil and alcohol 3. Symbols or letters

Muhammad al-Fazari
Arabic or Persian
Died 796 or 806

111 Muslims needed to know the true direction of Muhammad's birthplace. So scientists developed astronomical instruments to map the stars. The astrolabe was invented by astronomer Muhammad al-Fazari. It measured angles by sight, and skilled users could work out directions from the position of stars alone.

▶ Muslim astronomers mapped the stars and their movements very accurately.

112 Jabir ibn Hayyan (Geber) stirred and heated chemicals together in measured quantities to see how they interacted. Jabir also found he could purify liquids by boiling them and collecting the droplets of steam. This is called distillation and is used today for refining oil and alcoholic spirits.

113 Roman numerals were awkward to use for large numbers. So in the 8th century, after studying Indian Hindu numbers, al-Khwarizmi introduced the Arabic numerals we now use around the world. Roman numerals need seven figures to give a number as small as 38 (XXXVIII). With seven figures, Arabic numerals can give nearly ten million!

Jabir ibn Hayyan (Geber)
Persian 721–815

al-Khwarizmi
Arabic or Persian
c.780–850

▲ As well as distillation, Geber discovered acids that were strong enough to dissolve metals.

▶ Roman numerals were built up by adding lines. Arabic numerals use symbols for one to 10, which is simpler.

114 Al-Khwarizmi created the maths known as algebra. Algebra uses symbols or letters to replace unknown numbers in calculations. Mathematicians can work out the unknown numbers by putting the symbols in standard 'recipes' called equations. Algebra is part of nearly all scientific calculations.

115 When al-Khwarizmi's name was written in Latin it was spelt 'Algoritmi'. This name has given us the word 'algorithms'. Algorithms are logical step-by-step mathematical sequences, and it was al-Khwarizmi who first developed the idea. Algorithms are now the basis of all computer programs.

Ancient Roman	Modern Hindu-Arabic
I	1
II	2
III	3
IV	4
V	5
VI	6
VII	7
VIII	8
IX	9
X	10

Thinking again

116 In the 1400s, Islamic science reached Europe. The ideas of ancient Greece and Rome were rediscovered, and people like Leonardo da Vinci were excited. They realized that by studying the world, they might learn how it works.

▼ Leonardo was way ahead of his time, making models to study how rivers flowed.

117 You might think helicopters and cars are modern ideas — but Leonardo drew designs for them 500 years ago. His sketches for a hang-glider type flying machine are so detailed that experts recently built one for real — and found that it just about worked.

▼ A scientific genius, Leonardo made brilliant notes and drawings on everything from geology to flying machines.

118
Leonardo wrote to the Duke of Milan offering his services as an engineer. He had an idea for an armoured car or tank. Tanks were only first used in World War I (1914–1918). Yet there is a picture of one in Leonardo's notebooks from the 1480s.

119
To draw human figures accurately, artists studied the human body. To show the body's inner layers, Leonardo developed a way of drawing cross-sections and 3D versions of muscles.

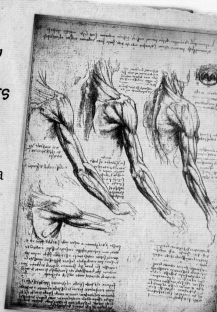

▶ Leonardo drew highly accurate diagrams of the human muscular system.

120
Early physicians learned about the body (often wrongly) from ancient books — especially those of Galen (129–199), a Roman doctor. Andreas Vesalius realized the only way to find out was to cut up real corpses (dead bodies). As he did this, he got artist Jan van Calcar to draw what he found. They made the first accurate book of human anatomy (the way the body is put together) in 1543.

▶ As Vesalius carefully cut up bodies, Jan van Calcar made drawings to build up an accurate guide to human anatomy.

Andreas Vesalius
Dutch 1514–1564

121
Many scientists studied in Padua in Italy in the 1500s, including English physician William Harvey. When Harvey returned to England, he studied how blood flowed through the body. He found that it doesn't flow to and fro like tides as Galen said. Instead it is pumped by the heart non-stop around the body through tubes called arteries and veins.

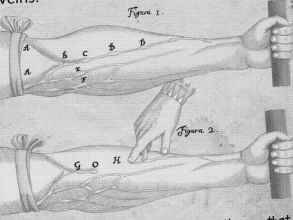

▲ Careful experiments showed William Harvey that blood flowed around the body again and again.

William Harvey
English 1578–1657

Moving heaven and Earth

122 Until the 1400s, most people thought the Earth was fixed in the middle of the Universe. They believed the Sun, Moon, planets and stars revolved around it. Astronomers came up with elaborate circle patterns to explain this. Then in 1514, Nicolas Copernicus realized the truth – the Earth goes around the Sun, along with the Moon and other planets.

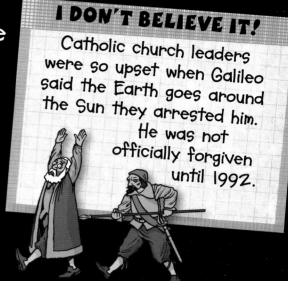

I DON'T BELIEVE IT!

Catholic church leaders were so upset when Galileo said the Earth goes around the Sun they arrested him. He was not officially forgiven until 1992.

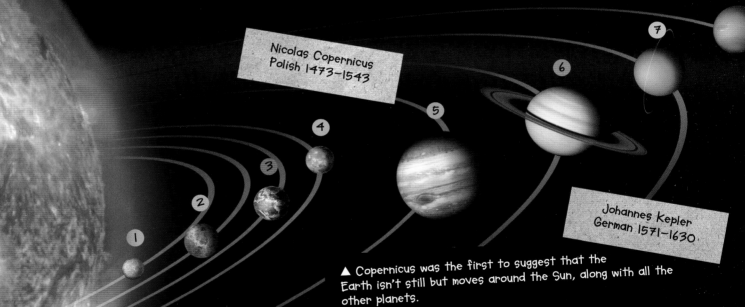

Nicolas Copernicus
Polish 1473–1543

Johannes Kepler
German 1571–1630

▲ Copernicus was the first to suggest that the Earth isn't still but moves around the Sun, along with all the other planets.

123 Copernicus' idea that the Earth goes around the Sun didn't seem to fit with observations. So even the cleverest astronomers thought he might be wrong. Their mistake was to assume that the planets' orbits (paths) are circular. German astronomer Johannes Kepler realized that their orbits are not circles, but an ellipse (oval). With elliptical orbits, the observations match Copernicus' idea exactly.

KEY

1 Mercury
2 Venus
3 Earth
4 Mars
5 Jupiter
6 Saturn
7 Uranus
8 Neptune

124 People wanted proof that Copernicus was right. The man to give it was Italian genius, Galileo Galilei. He invented the telescope so he could see the night sky better than anyone had before. Today, telescopes are revealing more and more to us about the Universe.

▼ Many church leaders did not believe that what Galileo showed them through the telescope was actually real.

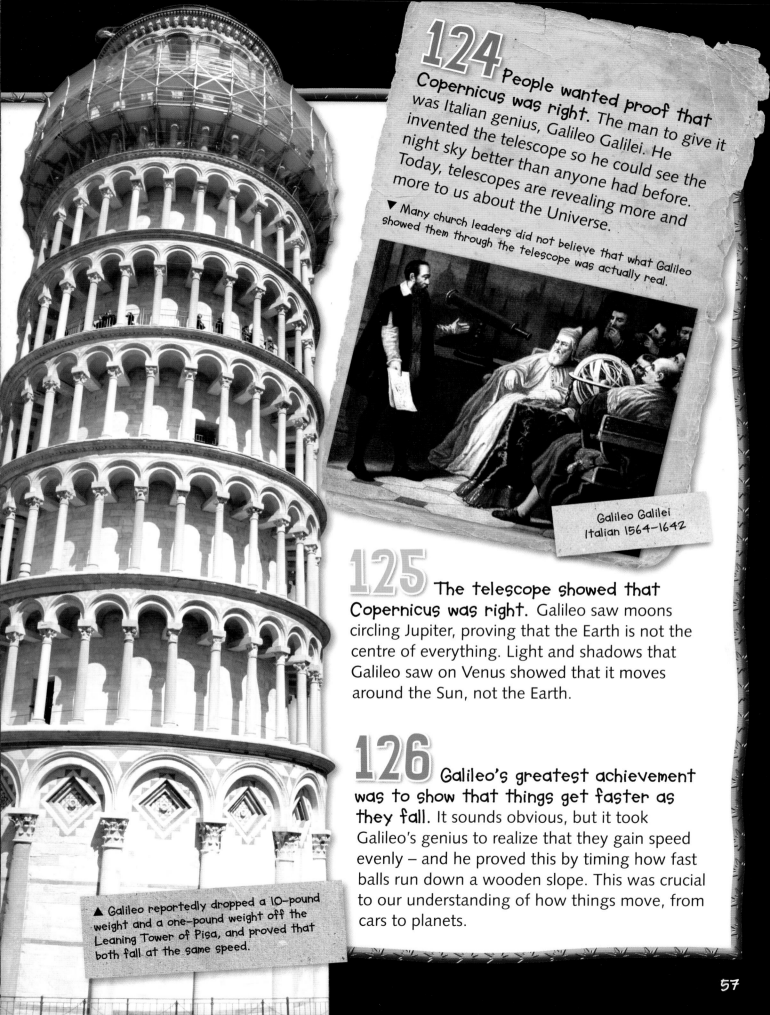

Galileo Galilei
Italian 1564–1642

125 The telescope showed that Copernicus was right. Galileo saw moons circling Jupiter, proving that the Earth is not the centre of everything. Light and shadows that Galileo saw on Venus showed that it moves around the Sun, not the Earth.

126 Galileo's greatest achievement was to show that things get faster as they fall. It sounds obvious, but it took Galileo's genius to realize that they gain speed evenly – and he proved this by timing how fast balls run down a wooden slope. This was crucial to our understanding of how things move, from cars to planets.

▲ Galileo reportedly dropped a 10–pound weight and a one–pound weight off the Leaning Tower of Pisa, and proved that both fall at the same speed.

Microbes and measures

Focusing screw

Screw to adjust height of specimen

Specimen pin

Metal plate

Lens

▲▶ Leeuwenhoek's microscope. He saw that even a tiny raindrop is teeming with microbes.

Anton von Leeuwenhoek
Dutch 1632–1723

128 Robert Hooke was another microscope pioneer and saw that living things are made from tiny 'parcels'. He called them cells, because to him they looked like tiny rows of rooms or cells that monks lived in. Hooke also invented the hearing aid and the anemometer (for measuring wind speed).

▶▼ Through his microscope, Hooke saw that living things are made up from tiny packages, which he named 'cells'.

127 No one knew there was life too small to see — until Anton von Leeuwenhoek looked through his microscope in the 1670s. Leeuwenhoek made his own microscope, with lenses that could magnify up to 270 times.

Christiaan Huygens
Dutch 1629–1695

Robert Hooke
English 1635–1703

129 Before the 1600s, people could only tell the time to within ten minutes. But in 1658 Christiaan Huygens perfected a clock that kept time with a swinging weight, or pendulum. It was the world's first accurate clock, so precise it could keep time to within a minute over a week.

◀ Huygens also worked out the maths of pendulums that helps us understand how planets move.

130 **Like Galileo, Huygens made his own telescope.** Peering through it, he saw that the planet Saturn had a moon, too, later called Titan. He also realized that what had looked to Galileo like ears on Saturn were part of a flat hoop or ring running around it.

▼ We now know that Saturn's rings are made up of tiny particles of water, ice and dust.

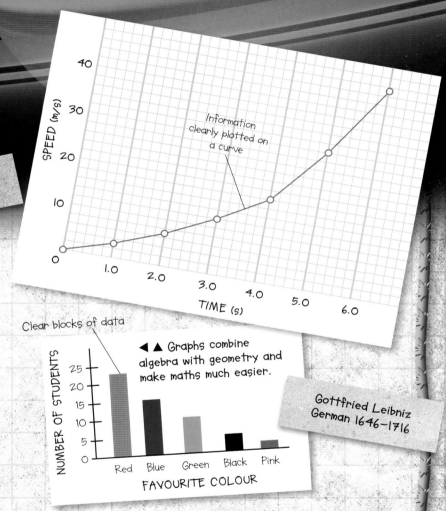

Information clearly plotted on a curve

René Descartes
French 1596–1650

131 **Descartes came up with the idea of graphs.** Graphs are a way of looking at things that are changing together. When something accelerates, both speed and time change. On a graph, you draw the changes as a simple line called a curve.

Clear blocks of data

◄▲ Graphs combine algebra with geometry and make maths much easier.

Gottfried Leibniz
German 1646–1716

I DON'T BELIEVE IT!

There are thought to be millions of types of bacteria, but no one knew they existed until Leeuwenhoek saw them through his microscope.

132 **Most things in nature move at varying speeds.** To study them, Isaac Newton and Gottfried Leibniz devised a kind of maths called calculus. Calculus helps you find out how fast something is moving at any one instant – a time so short that it seems to move no distance at all.

Motion man

Sir Isaac Newton
English 1643–1727

133 Isaac Newton discovered that every movement in the Universe obeys three rules, known as the Laws of Motion. They sum up what it takes to get something moving or to stop (1st Law), to make something move faster or slower, or change direction (2nd Law), and how the movement of one thing affects another (3rd Law).

LAW 1: An object won't move unless something forces it to. It will go on moving at the same speed and in the same direction unless forced to change. This is called inertia.

▶▲ Scientists can use these laws to work out everything – from the way a diver pushes off from a springboard to the rotation of a galaxy.

LAW 2: The greater the mass of an object, the more force is needed to make it speed up, slow down or change direction.

134 Newton also discovered gravity – the force of attraction between all matter. He knew that nothing strays from its course without being forced to. So when something starts to fall, it must be forced to. That force is gravity, the same force that holds planets in orbit around the Sun.

MARBLE MOTION

Demonstrate Newton's Third Law of Motion with marbles or the balls on a pool table. Roll one ball or marble into another – and watch how when they collide, one ball moves one way and the other ball moves the other way.

135 Early telescopes worked by using lenses to refract (bend) rays of light together. Newton used curved mirrors instead of lenses to throw light rays back on themselves, creating a compact, powerful telescope. Most telescopes today are Newtonian or 'reflecting' telescopes.

LAW 3: For every action, there is an equal opposite reaction – in other words, when something pushes off in one direction, the thing it's pushing from is pushed back with equal force in the opposite direction.

136 Sunlight is colourless or white — so where do all the colours come from? Newton realized that sunlight contains all the colours, mixed up. He proved it using a prism, a triangular block of glass.

▼ When sunlight shines through a prism, its rays are bent — each colour to a different degree. When the light emerges from the far side of the prism, it splits into a spectrum — all the colours of the rainbow.

137 Newton was the first modern scientist, but he wrote works of alchemy — a cross between science, magic and astrology. Alchemists wanted to find the 'philosopher's stone' (a substance that could turn metal to gold) and the 'elixir of life' (a liquid that keeps you young forever). They wrote in code to keep their work secret, and Newton's notebooks are impossible to understand.

Nature's secrets

138 Today, all living things are organized into clear groups — thanks to biologist Carolus Linnaeus. Before this, animals and plants were listed at best alphabetically. Since creatures have different names in different places, this led to chaos.

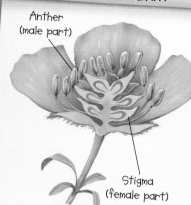

PARTS OF A FLOWERING PLANT

Anther (male part)

Stigma (female part)

▲ Linnaeus realized that flowering plants can be classified by the shape of their male and female parts.

Carolus Linnaeus
Swedish 1707–1778

139 Linnaeus gave all species a two-part scientific name in Latin. The first part is the group it belongs to, and the second is an individual name (like your name and family name, only with the family name first). For example, the swamp rabbit is *Sylvilagus aquaticus*.

James Hutton
Scottish 1726–1797

▲ A volcanic eruption is a short, sharp force of nature. James Hutton concluded that the landscape is shaped mostly by more gradual forces such as running rivers.

140 People once thought the Earth was just a few thousand years old and the entire landscape was shaped by a few short, huge disasters. But in his book *Theory of the Earth*, published in 1788, James Hutton showed how the Earth has been shaped gradually over millions of years by milder forces, such as running rivers.

HOMEMADE FOSSIL

Make your own fossil by pressing a snail shell or an old bone into tightly compressed fine sand. Take out the shell or bone, then pour runny plaster or wall filler into the mould left behind. Leave the plaster to set, then dig up your fossil!

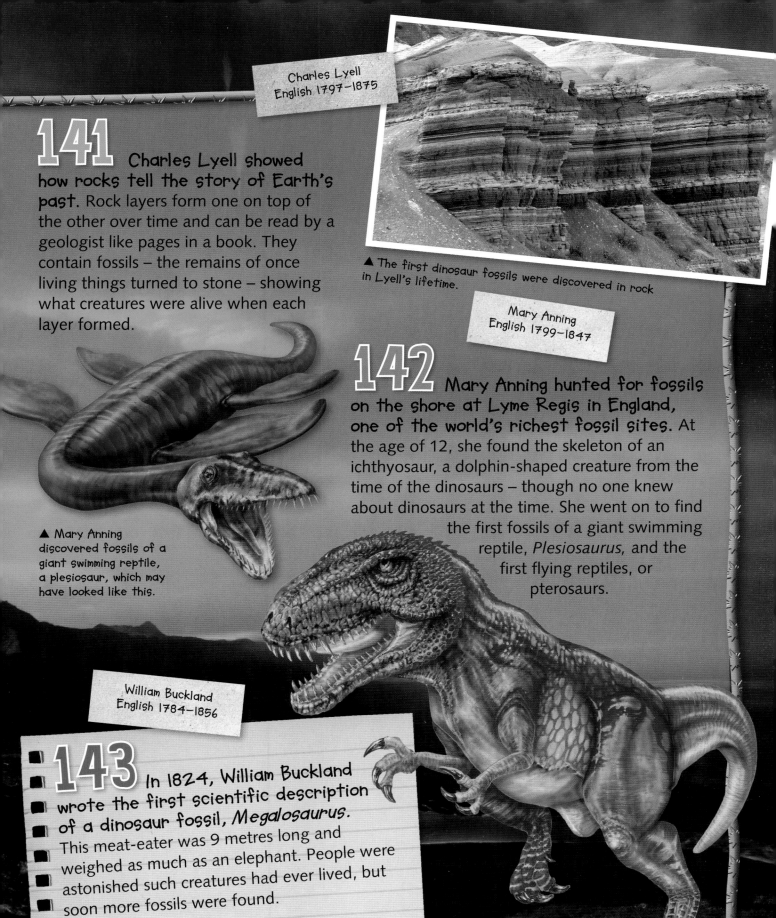

141

Charles Lyell showed how rocks tell the story of Earth's past. Rock layers form one on top of the other over time and can be read by a geologist like pages in a book. They contain fossils – the remains of once living things turned to stone – showing what creatures were alive when each layer formed.

▲ The first dinosaur fossils were discovered in rock in Lyell's lifetime.

142

Mary Anning hunted for fossils on the shore at Lyme Regis in England, one of the world's richest fossil sites. At the age of 12, she found the skeleton of an ichthyosaur, a dolphin-shaped creature from the time of the dinosaurs – though no one knew about dinosaurs at the time. She went on to find the first fossils of a giant swimming reptile, *Plesiosaurus*, and the first flying reptiles, or pterosaurs.

▲ Mary Anning discovered fossils of a giant swimming reptile, a plesiosaur, which may have looked like this.

143

In 1824, William Buckland wrote the first scientific description of a dinosaur fossil, *Megalosaurus*. This meat-eater was 9 metres long and weighed as much as an elephant. People were astonished such creatures had ever lived, but soon more fossils were found.

▶ Buckland named *Megalosaurus* in 1824. It was not until 1842 that the term 'dinosaur' was first used.

It's chemistry

Gas molecules

Plunger squeezes gas

Large volume of gas with low pressure

Medium volume of gas with medium pressure

Small volume of gas with high pressure

▲ When a gas is squeezed, the pressure increases in proportion. The more the gas is squeezed, the higher the pressure.

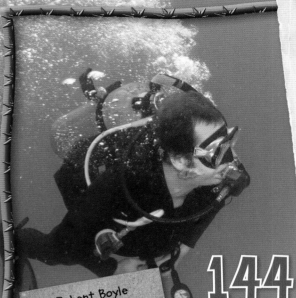

Robert Boyle
Irish 1627–1691

▲ Boyle's Law shows that the pressure of gases in a diver's suit and body rises as he descends, due to the weight of the water.

144 Robert Boyle was the first great chemist of modern times. With Boyle's Law, he showed that when a gas is compressed its pressure increases at the same rate. He also suggested that everything is made up from basic chemicals or 'elements', which can join together in different ways.

145 People once believed air was not a substance. But Antoine Lavoisier realized substances can exist in three different states – solid, liquid and gas – and if gases are substances, then so is air. He found air is a mix of gases, mostly nitrogen and oxygen.

146 Scientists used to think that everything that burns contained a substance called phlogiston. They thought that as something burned it lost phlogiston. Lavoisier found by careful weighing that tin gains weight when it burns, because it takes in oxygen. So phlogiston couldn't exist. Lavoisier had proved the importance of accurate measurement.

▼ Lavoisier showed that, like solid elements, two gases can join to make a new substance, or compound. Here he is experimenting with hydrogen and oxygen, to produce water.

Antoine Lavoisier
French 1743–1794

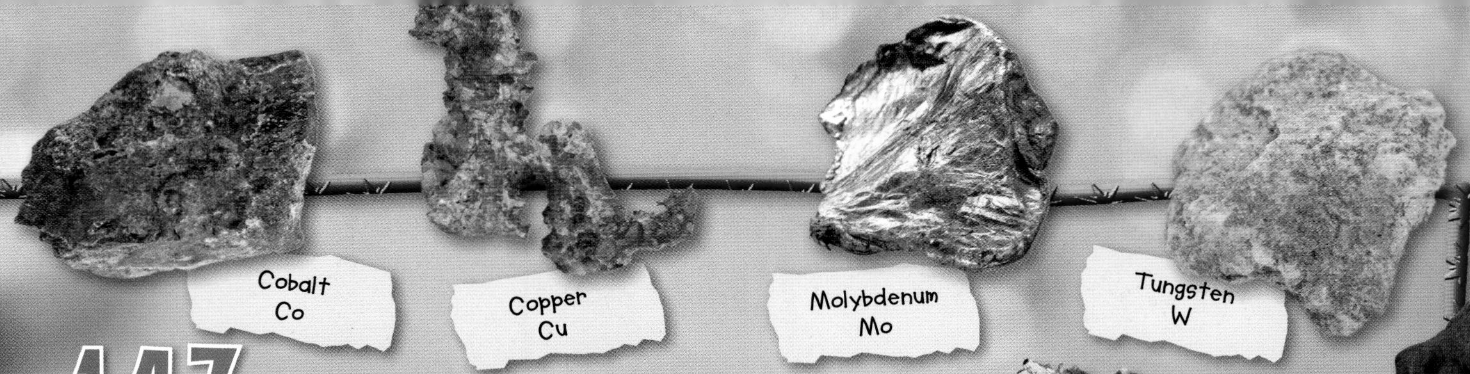

Cobalt
Co

Copper
Cu

Molybdenum
Mo

Tungsten
W

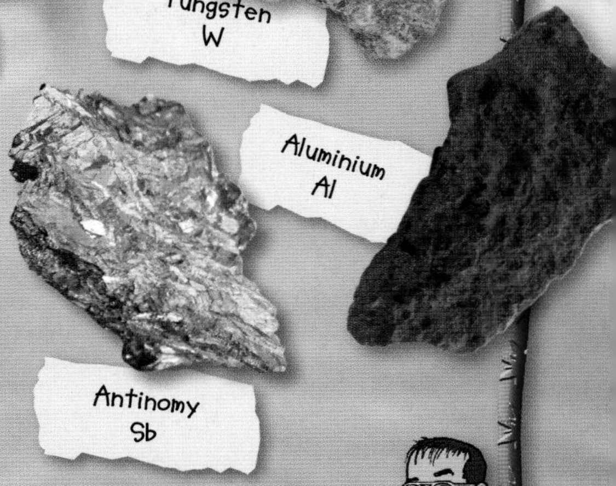

Aluminium
Al

Antinomy
Sb

▲▶ Minerals help to make up rocks. Each of these minerals contains a particular metal. The chemical symbols shown here are for each metal.

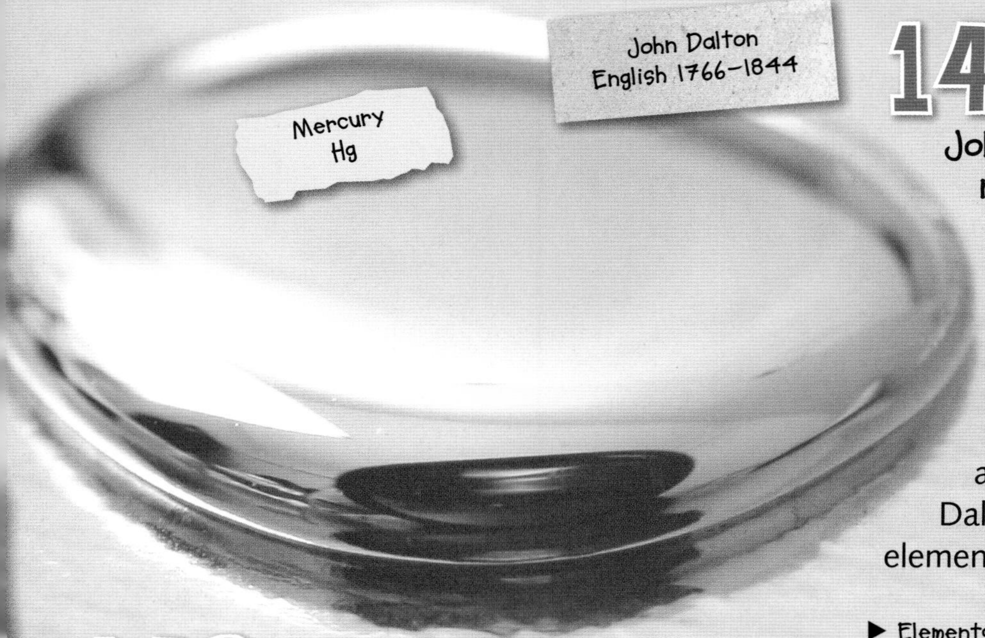

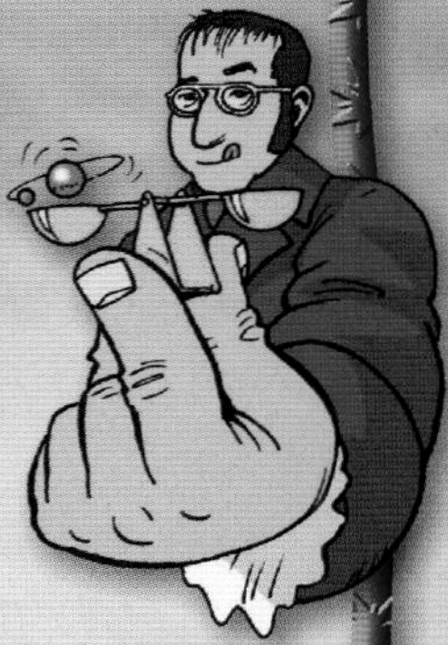

147 In 1787, Lavoisier introduced symbols for the different chemical elements. So oxygen is 'O' and hydrogen is 'H'. Lavoisier knew of less than 40 elements. Today, chemists use chemical formulae to identify compounds and the mix of elements of which they are composed. For example, water has the chemical symbol H_2O. This means it has two hydrogen (H) atoms to one oxygen (O).

Mercury
Hg

John Dalton
English 1766–1844

148 Chemist John Dalton realized elements are made from solid particles called atoms. Each element is made from atoms of a certain weight. He found hydrogen to be the lightest, so he assigned it an 'atomic weight' of 1. Dalton's atomic theory of the elements is central to chemistry.

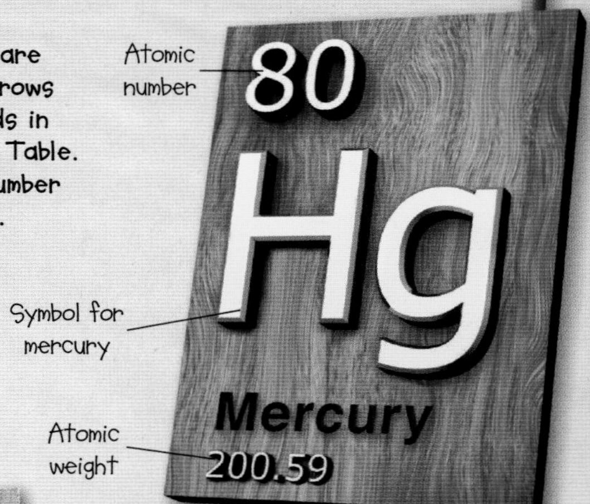

▶ Elements are arranged in rows called periods in the Periodic Table. Mecury is number 80, in row 6.

Atomic number

80

Hg

Symbol for mercury

Mercury

Atomic weight

200.59

149 In 1869, Dmitri Mendeleyev arranged the elements in a table in order of their atomic weight. He placed them from left to right in rows or 'periods' of seven that revealed a pattern. Elements in the same column (from top to bottom) have similar properties. All elements at one end of each row are reactive metals, while those at the other are unreactive gases.

Dmitri Mendeleyev
Russian 1834–1907

Sparks of genius

150
In the 1700s, scientists discovered that rubbing things together can give an electrical charge and may create a spark. Benjamin Franklin wondered if lightning was electrical too. He attached a key to a kite, which he flew during a thunderstorm, and got a similar spark from the key.

▼ A spark flew from the key on Franklin's kite, showing that lightning was electrical.

Benjamin Franklin
American 1706–1790

Luigi Galvani
Italian 1737–1798

151
Luigi Galvani made a dead frog's legs twitch with electricity. He believed, incorrectly, that electricity was made by animals' bodies. Alessandro Volta believed this was just a chemical reaction. In 1800, he used the reaction between 'sandwiches' of discs made of the metals copper and zinc in saltwater to create a battery.

Zinc

Copper

Wire

◄ The Voltaic pile battery was the first plentiful source of electricity.

Alessandro Volta
Italian 1745–1827

Hans Christiaan Øersted
Danish 1777–1851

152
No one realized electricity and magnetism were linked — until physicist Hans Øersted noticed something strange. During a lecture in 1820, he observed that when an electric current was switched on and off, a nearby compass needle swivelled. He went on to confirm with experiments that an electric current creates a magnetic field around it. This effect is known as electromagnetism.

153

Michael Faraday English 1791–1867

153 **Michael Faraday was fascinated by Øersted's discovery.** The following year he showed how the interreaction between a magnet and an electrical current can make a wire move. Faraday and others then went on to use this discovery to create the first electric motors.

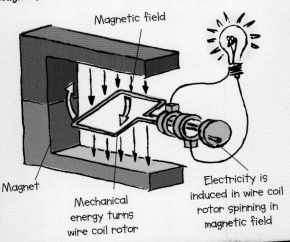

▼ Faraday found that when a wire moves near a magnet, an electric current is generated in it.

Magnetic field

Magnet

Mechanical energy turns wire coil rotor

Electricity is induced in wire coil rotor spinning in magnetic field

154 **In 1830, Faraday in London and Joseph Henry in New York found that magnets create electricity.** When a magnet is moved near an electric circuit, it creates a surge of electricity. Using this idea, machines could be built to generate lots of electricity.

Joseph Henry American 1797–1878

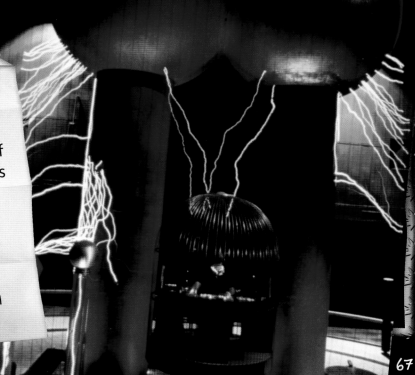

155 **Faraday's experiments with electricity convinced him that all types of electricity were basically the same.** It didn't matter if they were produced naturally in Earth's atmosphere in the form of lightning, artificially by chemical reactions in a battery, or by a rotating copper coil inside a magnetic field.

▶ Faraday showed how a cage of metal wire (known as a Faraday cage) could block electrical discharges and protect a person from lightning.

Life story

156 In 1830, Charles Darwin set out on a voyage around the world in the ship HMS *Beagle*. The journey lasted five years, and took in places such as the Galápagos Islands in the Pacific. Darwin recorded the huge range of wildlife he saw, which sowed the seeds of his theory of evolution.

157 Darwin's idea was that evolution (when species gradually change through time) occurs through 'natural selection'. Organisms are all born slightly different. Those born with differences that help them cope better with the conditions are more likely to survive and have offspring. Their special difference is 'naturally selected' and passed on, while others die out.

▼ Cut off from the mainland and from each other, the Galápagos Islands developed a unique range of creatures, helping Darwin develop his ideas.

▲ Perhaps Darwin's most famous example of natural selection is the Galápagos finch. Each species has evolved a unique beak shape to suit their diets.

SAN SALVADOR

FERNANDINA

SANTA CRUZ

SANTA FE

SAN CRISTOBAL

ISABELA

SANTA MARIA

ESPANOLA

Cormorants on these remote isles lost the ability to fly

Each island has evolved its own kind of giant tortoise

Native fur seals never stray far from the Galápagos shores

158 Darwin worked on his idea for 20 years. Naturalists sent him observations, and he received letters from animal breeders. Breeders said they could bring out certain characteristics by selecting the right animals to breed from. That's why there are so many different breeds of dogs.

▲ Darwin concluded that humans and apes, such as chimpanzees, gorillas and orang-utans, all share a common ancestor.

159 In 1858, Alfred Russel Wallace sent Darwin a letter suggesting, like Darwin, that evolution occurs by natural selection. They decided to publish their ideas together, so some say it was Wallace's idea too. But Darwin had already spent 20 years working out the details. In 1859 Darwin told the world about his theory in his book *On the Origin of Species*.

▼ Due to natural selection, light-coloured peppered moths are dying out. Darker specimens, which are better hidden on trees darkened by pollution, are more common.

160 Some religious people were upset by Darwin's ideas. They believed all species were created at once by God. They didn't like the idea that humans evolved from apes. The fuss eventually died down, and Darwin's theory is now widely accepted.

Alfred Russel Wallace
British 1823–1913

Thriving darker-coloured moth

Vanishing lighter-coloured moth

Cured!

161

People who survived the disease smallpox became immune to a second attack. This meant their bodies could resist the infection. Doctor Edward Jenner injected his gardener's son with cowpox, a milder disease, to see if it gave the same immunity. It did.

▲ By injecting his gardener's son with cowpox, Edward Jenner had taken the first step towards wiping out the killer disease smallpox.

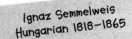

162

Before 1850, no one knew dirt in hospitals could spread killer germs. Countless patients died of infections. Doctor Ignaz Semmelweis asked students to wash their hands before dealing with patients. This act of simple hygiene helped reduce the number of deaths.

163

Surgeon Joseph Lister introduced soap to his operations to keep things spotlessly clean. Cleanliness cut infections during surgery dramatically, and antiseptic techniques are now a vital part of every operation.

◀ Lister invented a carbolic spray to limit infections during surgery.

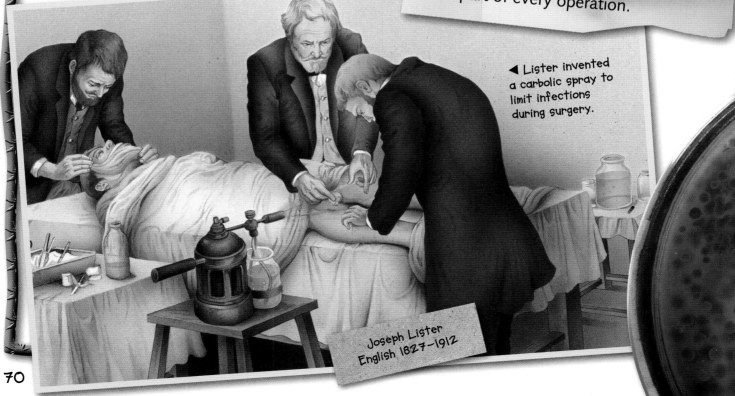

Joseph Lister
English 1827–1912

164 The idea that germs cause disease has been around for over 400 years. But it was Louis Pasteur who, with Robert Koch, proved the link in the 1870s. They showed how bacteria spread the sheep disease anthrax.

Louis Pasteur
French 1822–1895

▼ We now know many diseases are spread by microbes — mainly bacteria and viruses. In future they may be targeted by tiny 'nano-robots' placed inside our bodies.

Robert Koch
German 1843–1910

Paul Ehrlich
German 1854–1915

165 Paul Ehrlich believed diseases might be cured by targeting germs with chemical 'magic bullets.' He and student Sahachiro Hato searched for a chemical to kill the bacteria that caused the disease syphilis. They found one called arsphenamine, which wiped out the syphilis germ but left the patient almost unharmed.

Sahachiro Hato
Japanese 1873–1938

Alexander Fleming
Scottish 1881–1955

166 In 1928, Alexander Fleming saw a clue that led to the miracle drugs antibiotics. He was culturing (growing) bacteria in dishes in his lab, when he saw that mould growing on one neglected dish had killed the bacteria. Fleming realized that the mould, called *Penicillium notatum*, could be harnessed to fight disease.

◄ Ten years after Fleming discovered the bacteria-killing mould, Howard Florey (1898–1968) and Ernst Chain (1906–1977) created the first antibiotic drug, penicillin.

Dangerous rays

167 In 1886, Heinrich Hertz proved that an electromagnetic current spreads as waves. He made a flickering electric spark jump a gap in an electrical circuit. As the spark flickered, it radiated waves, which set another spark flickering in sync in an aerial receiver. Hertz had discovered radio waves.

Heinrich Hertz
German 1857–1894

② High voltage current jumps a gap in an electric circuit and creates a spark

③ Spark sends out electromagnetic waves

④ Waves induce a tiny spark in aerial receiver

① Coil produces high voltage current

▲ Hertz's experiments with electricity and electromagnetic waves led to the development of the radio.

I DON'T BELIEVE IT!

Before people realized how dangerous it was, radium was added to products such as toothpaste and hair cream to give them a healthy glow.

▼ We now know that the cathode rays in Crookes' glass tube were actually made up of tiny electrical particles.

Cathode rays

Cathode terminal

Anode terminal

Mask

Shadow

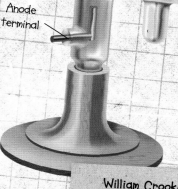

168 In the 1870s, William Crookes made a glass tube with nearly all the air sucked out of it. When connected to an electric current, the glass tube glowed. This was because electric charge flowed between the terminals, sending out electromagnetic radiation, which Crookes called cathode rays. A metal mask inside the tube cast a shadow, showing that the rays travelled in straight lines.

William Crookes
English 1832–1919

Wilhelm Röntgen
German 1845–1923

169

In 1895, Wilhelm Röntgen found that even when he covered a Crookes tube, its rays still made a nearby screen glow. Some rays must be shining through the cover. He tried putting other objects in front of the rays (which he called X-rays) and eventually placed his wife's hand. The rays passed through flesh, but were blocked by bone. Röntgen replaced the screen with photo paper and took the first X-ray photo of his wife's hand.

▼ As well as bone, Röntgen discovered that X-rays were blocked by the metal of his wife's jewellery, and a compass!

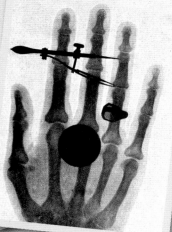

Henri Becquerel
French 1852–1908

170

Henri Becquerel found that uranium crystals left on photo paper in a drawer made a photo of themselves. They were releasing or 'radiating' their own energy. He had discovered radioactivity – radiation so energetic it breaks up atoms. This kind of radiation is quite different from electromagnetic radiation and is used to make nuclear bombs.

◄ Marie Curie was the first woman to be awarded a Nobel Prize, in 1903 for physics. She was awarded it again, this time in chemistry, in 1911.

Pierre Curie
French 1859–1906

171

Pierre and Marie Curie were fascinated by radioactivity. They discovered two new radioactive elements, radium and polonium. In 1903, they were awarded the Nobel Prize for their work. Marie Curie died from cancer caused by exposure to radioactivity.

Marie Curie
Polish 1867–1934

Atomic science

Sir Joseph John (JJ) Thomson
English 1856–1940.

172 **Scientists once thought atoms were the smallest particles.** In 1897, JJ Thomson noticed how magnets bent rays from a cathode ray tube. He realized the rays were streams of particles, much smaller than an atom. Thomson wrongly believed these particles or 'electrons' split off from atoms like currents off a bun.

173 **Ernest Rutherford found that radioactivity is the result of atoms breaking up into different atoms, sending out streams of 'alpha' and 'beta' particles.** In 1911, he fired streams of alpha particles at gold foil. Most went straight through, but a few bounced back, pushed by the nuclei inside the gold foil atoms. He realized that atoms aren't solid, but largely empty space with a tiny, dense nucleus (core).

Sir Ernest Rutherford
New Zealand-born British
1871–1937

▶ Fortunately, all nuclear explosions since the attack on Japan in 1945 have been tests.

174 **In 1912, Niels Bohr suggested that different kinds of atom had a certain number of electrons.** He thought they buzzed around an atom's nucleus at varying distances, like planets around the Sun. Atoms give out light and lose energy when electrons fall closer to the nucleus. When atoms absorb light, the electrons jump further out.

▶ We now know that electrons are like fuzzy clouds of energy rather than planets.

Niels Bohr
Danish 1885–1962

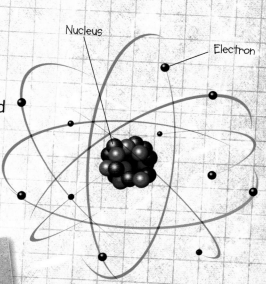

Nucleus

Electron

James Chadwick
English 1891–1974

175

In 1918 Rutherford split atoms for the first time. He fired alpha particles at nitrogen gas and found that hydrogen nuclei chipped off the nitrogen nuclei. He realized that all atomic nuclei are clusters of hydrogen nuclei, which he called protons. Fourteen years later, James Chadwick discovered nuclei also have another kind of particle in the nucleus – the neutron.

176

Enrico Fermi fired neutrons at a uranium atom, to see if they'd stick to form a bigger atom. Instead, the uranium atom split into two smaller atoms and released more neutrons, and heat and light energy. Fermi realized that if these neutrons spun off to split more uranium atoms a 'chain reaction' of splitting could occur.

Enrico Fermi
Italian–American
1901–1954

① Neutron fired at nucleus of Uranium atom

② Nucleus splits in two

④ More neutrons released

Uranium atom

③ Energy released

⑤ Chain reaction occurs

177

During World War II (1939–1945) Fermi created a chain reaction of nuclear splitting, or 'fission'. This unleashed energy to create an incredibly powerful bomb. At Los Alamo, New Mexico, Robert Oppenheimer used this idea to make the first nuclear bombs, which were dropped on the Japanese cities of Hiroshima and Nagasaki in August 1945, killing thousands of people outright.

Robert Oppenheimer
American 1904–1967

▲ Enrico Fermi showed how a chain reaction of an atom splitting could begin with the impact of just a single neutron.

BOWLING REACTION!

Ask an older relative to take you ten-pin bowling. It's not just fun, it'll show you how a nuclear chain reaction can work, especially if you are lucky enough to strike ten. The ball may only hit one pin directly, but as that pin falls, it can knock down all the rest in turn.

Space and time weirdness

178 In 1900, Max Planck worked out that heat is not radiated in a smooth flow, but in tiny chunks of energy that he called quanta. Albert Einstein realized that all radiation works like this – and that chunks of energy are particles. So a ray of light is streams of particles, not just waves, as everyone thought.

Albert Einstein
German 1879–1955

TRUE OR FALSE?

1. A ray of light is made up of particles.
2. The speed of light can vary.
3. Gravity bends space and time.
4. Paul Dirac's theory was called quantum engines.

Answers:
1.True 2. False, the speed of light is always the same 3. True 4. False, it was called quantum mechanics

▲ With his theories of relativity, Einstein overturned our understanding of the nature of time and space.

179 Speed is always measured compared to something, so the speed of an object varies depending on what you compare it to. In 1887, Einstein showed that light is special – it travels the same speed no matter how you measure it. Speed is the distance something moves through space in a certain time. If light's speed is fixed, Einstein realized that time and space must vary instead. So time and space are not fixed – they are relative and can be distorted. This is Einstein's theory of special relativity.

180 Einstein's theory of special relativity has weird effects for things travelling near the speed of light. For example, time on board a spacecraft travelling near the speed of light would seem to run slower, and the spacecraft would appear to shrink in length and get heavier.

Black hole

► In his theory of general relativity, Einstein showed that gravity bends space—time, leading scientists to predict the existence of black holes.

Waves of gravity (white lines) distorted by star and planet

STAR

EARTH

181 Anything with mass bends time and space around it. This is what Einstein showed in his general theory of relativity. The more massive something is, the greater the distortion. This is how gravity works. It pulls things together just by bending the space and time between them. By bending space and time, gravity can even bend a light ray.

Scanning head of STM

182 In the 1920s, scientists found that tiny particles, or quanta, didn't behave according to Newton's laws. Paul Dirac came up with a new theory, called quantum mechanics, which he combined with Einstein's special relativity theory. In his theory, Dirac was able to explain the properties and behaviour of quanta.

▼ A Scanning Tunnelling Microscope (STM) can magnify atoms, such as in this DNA sample.

Scanned surface

Stream of electrons

Paul Dirac English 1902–1984

▲ Quantum mechanics is used in modern technology, such as scanning tunnelling microscopes. These microscopes use streams of tiny electrons to create 3D images of atomic surfaces.

Star gazers

▶ Henrietta Leavitt discovered how the brightest cepheid stars take longest to vary.

183 A century ago, astronomers began to wonder if faint clouds in space called nebulae were actually distant galaxies. But were the stars within them really dim or just far away? To find out, astronomers looked for stars of varying brightness called cepheids. Slow varying cepheids are bright, so if they look dim, they must be far away.

▶ Andromeda was the first galaxy identified using cepheids.

Edwin Hubble
American 1889–1953

▶ Edwin Hubble making observations at the Mount Wilson telescope in California, USA.

184 In 1923, Edwin Hubble spotted a cepheid in the Andromeda nebula. It took a month to vary in brightness, so by Leavitt's scale it had to be 7000 times brighter than the Sun – and a million trillion kilometres away. So Andromeda must be a separate galaxy. Astronomers know now it is just one of 500 billion or so!

185 In 1931, Hubble found that the further away galaxies are, the redder they are. They are redder or 'red-shifted' because light waves are stretched out behind an object that is zooming away from us, just like sound drops in pitch after a car speeds past. So, the further a galaxy is from Earth, the faster it is moving away from us.

186 If galaxies are speeding apart now, they must have been closer together in the past. So the Universe is expanding. In the 1920s, Alexander Friedmann and Georges Lemaître suggested that the Universe was once just a tiny point that swelled like a giant explosion. One critic called the idea the Big Bang, and the name stuck.

187 Although the Big Bang theory caught on, there wasn't much proof. Then Arno Penzias and Robert Wilson picked up a faint buzz of radio signals from all over the sky. Astronomers believe that this buzz, called the Cosmic Microwave Background, is the faint afterglow of the Big Bang.

Robert Woodrow Wilson
American Born 1936

Arno Penzias
German–American
Born 1933

Alexander Friedmann
Russian 1888–1925

QUIZ

1. What was the first galaxy to be discovered beyond the Milky Way?
2. What is the theory of the origin of the Universe called?
3. What were pulsars jokingly called?

Answers:
1. The Andromeda Galaxy
2. The Big Bang
3. Little green men

▲ When Burnell first detected the radio pulses from pulsars, the stars were jokingly called 'little green men'.

Dame Jocelyn Bell Burnell
Northern Irish Born 1943

188 In 1967, Jocelyn Bell Burnell picked up strange radio pulses from certain stars. These pulsing stars, or pulsars, are actually tiny stars spinning at incredible speeds. They were once giant stars that have since collapsed to make a super-dense star just a few kilometres across.

Plan for life

189 Gregor Mendel wanted to know why some living things look like their parents and why others look different. In the 1860s, he experimented with pea flowers and their pollen to see which ones gave green peas and which ones gave yellow. Characteristics such as colour, he suggested, are passed to offspring by factors – which we now call genes.

▼ Chromosomes are the X-shaped bundles of DNA coiled up in the nucleus of a living cell.

Cell

Thomas Hunt Morgan
American 1866–1945

190 In the 1900s, Thomas Hunt Morgan experimented with fruit flies. He showed that genes are linked to tiny bundles in living cells called chromosomes. By removing materials from a bacterial cell one by one, Oswald Avery later found the one material it needed to pass on characteristics – DNA.

Cell nucleus contains chromosomes

Oswald Avery
Canadian-American
1877–1955

Rosalind Franklin
English 1920–1958

▲ The characteristics in this family group are clear to see, and have been passed on by DNA.

191 Scientists thought DNA's ability to pass on characteristics lay in its shape. Inspired by X-rays taken by Rosalind Franklin, Francis Crick and James Watson worked out in 1953 that the DNA molecule is a double helix (spiral). It's like a twisted rope ladder with two long strands either side linked by thousands of 'rungs'.

James Watson
American Born 1928

Francis Crick
English 1916–2004

◀ Every structure in the human body is created according to instructions to make proteins given by DNA.

Double spiral of DNA

Chromosome

A gene is a section of DNA

Chemical bases make up the rungs of DNA

Marshall Nirenberg
American 1927–2010

Har Gobind Khorana
Indian–American
1922–2011

Robert Holley
American 1922–1993

Arthur Kornberg
American 1918–2007

Werner Arber
Swiss Born 1929

Stanley Cohen
American Born 1922

192 **DNA's secret lies in the sequence of four chemical bases that make up its rungs.** The sequence creates a code, telling the cell to make different proteins. A gene is just the sequence that gives a particular protein. Marshall Nirenberg, Har Gobind Khorana and Robert Holley went to work to find out which sequence gave which protein. By 1966 they had worked out the entire code.

▶ By changing its DNA, scientists may be able to 'program' the mosquito that causes malaria to stop breeding.

193 **In the 1950s, Arthur Kornberg and Werner Arber found how to chemically copy, cut and paste segments of DNA.** Then Stanley Cohen showed how this rewritten DNA could be inserted into bacteria using little DNA snippets called plasmids. In 1972, Cohen inserted plasmids with rewritten toad DNA into bacteria to make the first genetically modified organisms.

◀ Identical twins are natural clones.

194 **Most animals have a mix of DNA from both parents, but the DNA of clones is exactly the same.** Cloning occurs naturally when bacteria divide. In 1996, Ian Wilmut took DNA from one sheep and placed it in the egg of another to create the first artificially cloned mammal, a sheep named Dolly.

Ian Wilmut
English Born 1944

Frontiers of science

196 By creating the World Wide Web in 1989, Tim Berners-Lee transformed the way the world communicates. The World Wide Web made the Internet accessible to everyone, anywhere in the world. It worked by turning computer output into web pages that could be read and displayed by any computer.

▲ Hawking suggested that the Big Bang might be a black hole in reverse, expanding from a singularity.

195 Stephen Hawking's work on black holes in space changed our understanding of the Universe. Black holes are places where gravity is so powerful that it draws in even light. At the centre is a minute point called a singularity.

197 Light is the fastest thing in the Universe. But in 2001 Lene Vestergaard Hau slowed it to a standstill by shining it through sodium atoms in a special cold state called a Bose-Einstein Condensate (BEC). In a BEC, atoms are so inactive there is nothing for particles of light to interact with, forcing them to slow down.

Brian Greene
American Born 1963

Michio Kaku
American Born 1947

Craig Venter
American Born 1946

198 Brian Greene and Michio Kaku are working on a theory that ties together all our ideas about the Universe, matter and energy. They believe everything is made of tiny strings of energy called superstrings. Just as a violin string can make different notes, so a superstring creates particles by vibrating in different ways.

▲ In 2010, Venter created the world's first man-made living cell.

199 Craig Venter was one of many scientists involved in mapping the entire sequence of genes in human DNA. He is also sampling the oceans for micro-organisms to see just how varied DNA is.

200 Scientists explain how forces such as electromagnetic radiation are transmitted by tiny messenger particles known as bosons. But they don't know why things are heavy and have mass, and why they take force to get going and stop. Peter Higgs suggested it could be down to a mystery particle now called the Higgs boson.

▼ Scientists are trying to find the Higgs boson with a massive underground machine at CERN in Switzerland, where they smash atoms together at incredible speeds.

Peter Higgs
English Born 1929

QUIZ

1. What would you find at the centre of a black hole?
2. What's the slowest speed light can travel?
3. Where is CERN?

Answers:
1. A singularity 2. A complete stop 3. Switzerland

HUMAN BODY

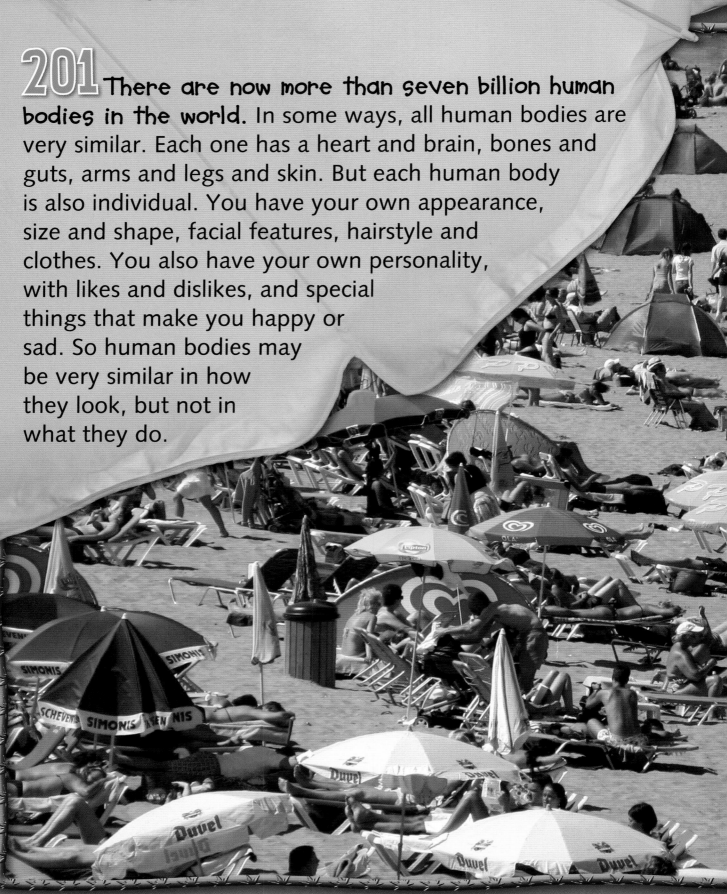

201 **There are now more than seven billion human bodies in the world.** In some ways, all human bodies are very similar. Each one has a heart and brain, bones and guts, arms and legs and skin. But each human body is also individual. You have your own appearance, size and shape, facial features, hairstyle and clothes. You also have your own personality, with likes and dislikes, and special things that make you happy or sad. So human bodies may be very similar in how they look, but not in what they do.

▲ We tend to notice small differences on the outside of human bodies, such as height, width, hair colour and clothes. This allows us to recognize our family and friends.

Baby body

Successful sperm

Egg cell

202
A full-grown human body is made of billions of microscopic parts, called cells. But in the beginning, the body is a single cell, smaller than this full stop. Yet it contains all the instructions, known as genes, for the whole body to grow and develop.

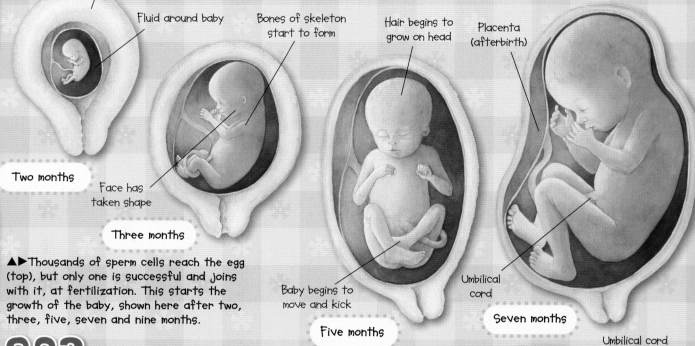

Wall of uterus

Fluid around baby

Bones of skeleton start to form

Hair begins to grow on head

Placenta (afterbirth)

Two months

Face has taken shape

Three months

▲▶Thousands of sperm cells reach the egg (top), but only one is successful and joins with it, at fertilization. This starts the growth of the baby, shown here after two, three, five, seven and nine months.

Baby begins to move and kick

Umbilical cord

Five months

Seven months

203
The body begins when an egg cell inside the mother joins up with sperm from the father. The egg cell splits into two cells, then into four cells, then eight, and so on. The bundle of cells embeds itself in the mother's womb (uterus), which protects and nourishes it. Soon there are thousands of cells, then millions, forming a tiny embryo. After two months the embryo has grown into a tiny baby, as big as your thumb, with arms, legs, eyes, ears and a mouth.

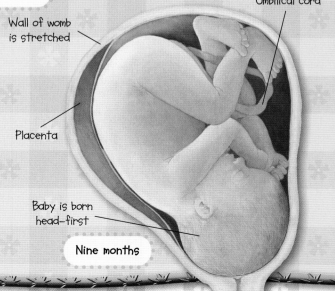

Umbilical cord

Wall of womb is stretched

Placenta

Baby is born head-first

Nine months

Cervix (neck of womb)

204
After nine months in the womb, the baby is ready to be born. Strong muscles in the walls of the womb tighten, or contract. They push the baby through the opening, or neck of the womb, called the cervix, and along the birth canal. The baby enters the outside world.

205
A newborn baby may be frightened and usually starts to cry. Inside the womb it was warm, wet, dark, quiet and cramped. Outside there are lights, noises, voices, fresh air and room to stretch. The crying is also helpful to start the baby breathing, using its own lungs.

206
Being born can take an hour or two – or a whole day or two. It is very tiring for both the baby and its mother. After birth, the baby starts to feel hungry and it feeds on its mother's milk. Finally, mother and baby settle down for a rest and some sleep.

I DON'T BELIEVE IT!
The human body never grows as fast again as it does during the first weeks in the womb. If the body kept growing at that rate, every day for 50 years, it would be bigger than the biggest mountain in the world!

▲ Once the baby is settled it is time for its mother to admire her newborn and rest.

The growing body

207 A new baby just seems to eat, sleep and cry. It feeds on milk when hungry and sleeps when tired. Also, it cries when it is too hot, too cold, or when its nappy needs changing.

208 A new baby is not totally helpless. It can do simple actions called reflexes, to help it survive. If something touches the baby's cheek, it turns its head to that side and tries to suck. If the baby hears a loud noise, it opens its eyes wide, throws out its arms and cries for help. If something touches the baby's hand and fingers, it grasps tightly.

209 A new baby looks, listens, touches and quickly learns. Gradually it starts to recognize voices, faces and places. After about six weeks, it begins to smile. Inside the body, the baby's brain is learning very quickly. The baby soon knows that if it laughs, people will laugh back and if it cries, someone will come to look after it.

WHAT HAPPENS WHEN?

Most babies learn to do certain actions in the same order. The order is mixed up here.
Can you put it right?

walk, crawl, roll over, sit up, smile, stand

Answers:
smile, roll over, sit up, crawl, stand, walk

▼ In the grasping reflex, the baby tightly holds anything that touches its hand or fingers. Its grip is surprisingly strong!

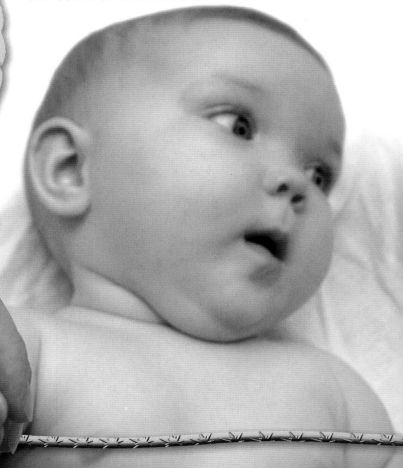

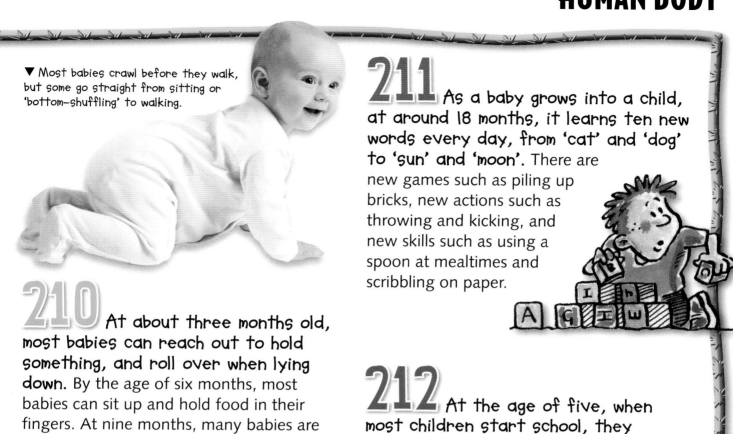

▼ Most babies crawl before they walk, but some go straight from sitting or 'bottom-shuffling' to walking.

211 As a baby grows into a child, at around 18 months, it learns ten new words every day, from 'cat' and 'dog' to 'sun' and 'moon'. There are new games such as piling up bricks, new actions such as throwing and kicking, and new skills such as using a spoon at mealtimes and scribbling on paper.

210 At about three months old, most babies can reach out to hold something, and roll over when lying down. By the age of six months, most babies can sit up and hold food in their fingers. At nine months, many babies are crawling well and perhaps standing up. By their first birthday, many babies are learning to walk and starting to talk.

▼ Playing is lots of fun, but it's learning too, as children develop control over the muscles in their fast-growing bodies.

212 At the age of five, when most children start school, they continue to learn an amazing amount. This includes thinking or mental skills such as counting and reading, and precise movements such as writing and drawing. They learn out of the classroom too – how to play with friends and share.

On the body's outside

213 Skin's surface is made of tiny cells that have filled up with a hard, tough substance called keratin, and then died. So when you look at a human body, most of what you see is 'dead'! The cells get rubbed off as you move, have a wash and get dry.

214 Skin rubs off all the time, and grows all the time too. Just under the surface, living cells make more new cells that gradually fill with keratin, die and move up to the surface. It takes about four weeks from a new skin cell being made to when it reaches the surface and is rubbed off. This upper layer of skin is called the epidermis.

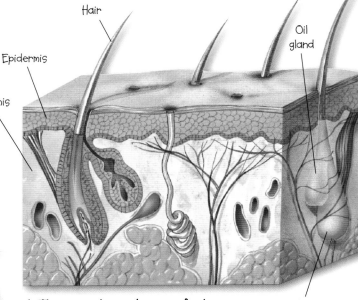

Hair

Oil gland

Epidermis

Dermis

Hair follicle

▲ This view shows skin magnified (enlarged) about 50 times.

▲ Lots of dead skin is removed without you realizing when you dry yourself after a shower.

215 Skin's lower layer, the dermis, is thicker than the epidermis. It is made of tiny, bendy, thread-like fibres of the substance collagen. The dermis also contains small blood vessels, tiny sweat glands, and micro-sensors that detect touch.

216

One of skin's important jobs is to protect the body. It stops the delicate inner parts from being rubbed, knocked or scraped. Skin also prevents body fluids from leaking away and it keeps out dirt and germs.

Safety helmet protects head and brain

Elbow-pads cushion fall

Gloves save fingers from scrapes and breaks

Knee-pads prevent hard bumps

▲ Skin is tough, but it sometimes needs help to protect the body. Otherwise it, and the body parts beneath, may get damaged.

217

Skin helps to keep the body at the same temperature. If you become too hot, sweat oozes onto your skin and, as it dries, draws heat from the body. Also, the blood vessels in the lower layer of skin widen, to lose more heat through the skin. This is why a hot person looks sweaty and red in the face.

218

Skin gives us our sense of touch. Millions of microscopic sensors in the lower layer of skin, the dermis, are joined by nerves to the brain. These sensors detect different kinds of touch, from a light stroke to heavy pressure, heat or cold, and movement. Pain sensors detect when skin is damaged. Ouch!

SENSITIVE SKIN

You will need:
a friend   sticky-tack
two used matchsticks   ruler

1. Press some sticky-tack on the end of the ruler. Press two matchsticks into the sticky-tack, standing upright, about 1 centimetre apart.

2. Make your friend look away. Touch the back of their hand with both matchstick ends. Ask your friend: 'Is that one matchstick or two?' Sensitive skin can detect both ends.

3. Try this at several places, such as on the finger, wrist, forearm, neck and cheek.

Hair and nails

219 There are about 120,000 hairs on the head, called scalp hairs. There are also eyebrow hairs and eyelash hairs. Grown-ups have hairs in the armpits and between the legs, and men have hairs on the face. And everyone, even a baby, has tiny hairs all over the body – 5 to 10 million of them!

Blonde wavy hair is the result of carotene from an oval hair follicle

Black curly hair is the result of black melanin from a flat hair follicle

Straight red hair is the result of red melanin from a round hair follicle

◀ Hair contains pigments (coloured substances) – mainly melanin (dark brown) and some carotene (yellowish). Different amounts of pigments, and the way their tiny particles are spread out, cause different hair colours.

220 Each hair grows from a deep pit in the skin, called a follicle. The hair is only alive where it gets longer, at its base or root, in the bottom of the follicle. The rest of the hair, called the shaft, is like the surface of the skin – hard, tough, dead and made of keratin. Hair helps to protect the body, especially where it is thicker and longer on the head. It also helps to keep the body warm in cold conditions.

Straight black hair is the result of black melanin from a round follicle

221 Scalp hairs get longer by about 3 millimetres each week, on average. Eyebrow hairs grow more slowly. No hairs live forever. Each one grows for a time, then it falls out, and its follicle has a 'rest' before a new hair sprouts. This is happening all the time, so the body always has some hairs on each part.

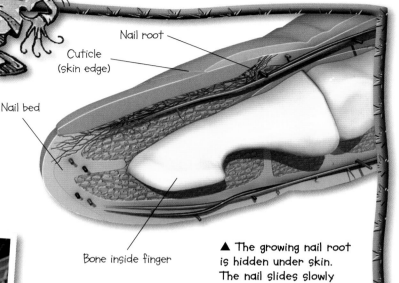

Nail root

Cuticle
(skin edge)

Nail bed

Bone inside finger

222 Nails, like hairs, grow at their base (the nail root) and are made of keratin. They grow faster in summer than in winter, and faster by day than by night. Nails lengthen by about half a millimetre, on average, each week.

▲ Nails make the fingertips stronger and more rigid for pressing hard on guitar strings. Slightly longer nails pluck the strings.

▲ The growing nail root is hidden under skin. The nail slides slowly along the nail bed.

223 Nails have many uses, from peeling off sticky labels to plucking guitar strings or scratching an itch. They protect and stiffen the ends of the fingers, where there are nerves that give us our sense of touch.

I DON'T BELIEVE IT!

A scalp hair grows for up to five years before it falls out and gets replaced. Left uncut during this time, it would be about one metre long. But some people have unusual hair that grows faster and for longer. Each hair can reach more than 5 metres in length before dropping out.

▶ Keeping your nails clean is very important. If you don't, germs can build up under your nails and make you ill.

The bony body

224 **Without bones, the body would be as floppy as a jellyfish!** Bones do many jobs. The long bones in the arms work like levers to reach out the hands. The finger bones grasp and grip. Bones protect softer body parts. The dome-like skull protects the brain. The ribs shield the lungs and heart. Bones also produce blood cells, as explained on the opposite page.

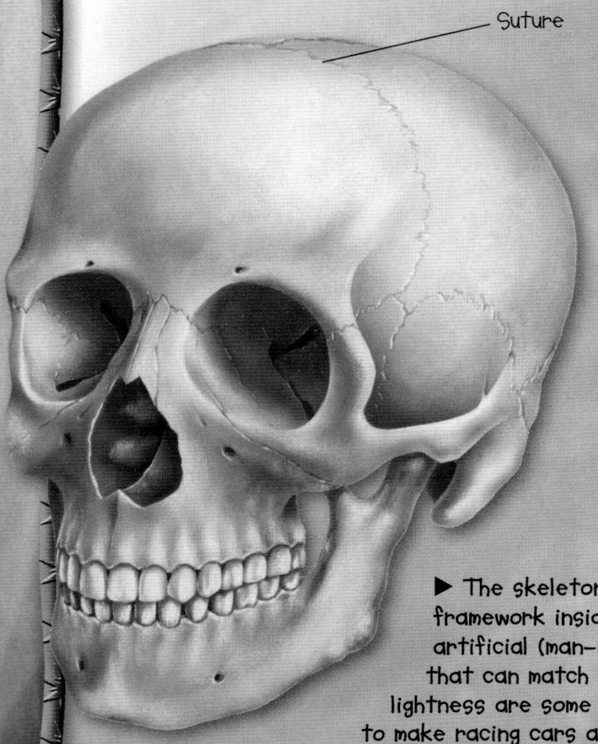

Cranium (skull)

Mandible (lower jaw)

Sternum (breastbone)

Clavicle (collarbone)

Rib

Humerus

Vertebra (backbone)

Ulna

Radius

Pelvis (hip bone)

Femur (thigh bone)

Patella (kneecap)

Tibia

Fibula

Heel bone

Toe bone

Suture

◄ The skull has deep bowls for the eyes, and small holes where nerves pass through to join the brain inside.

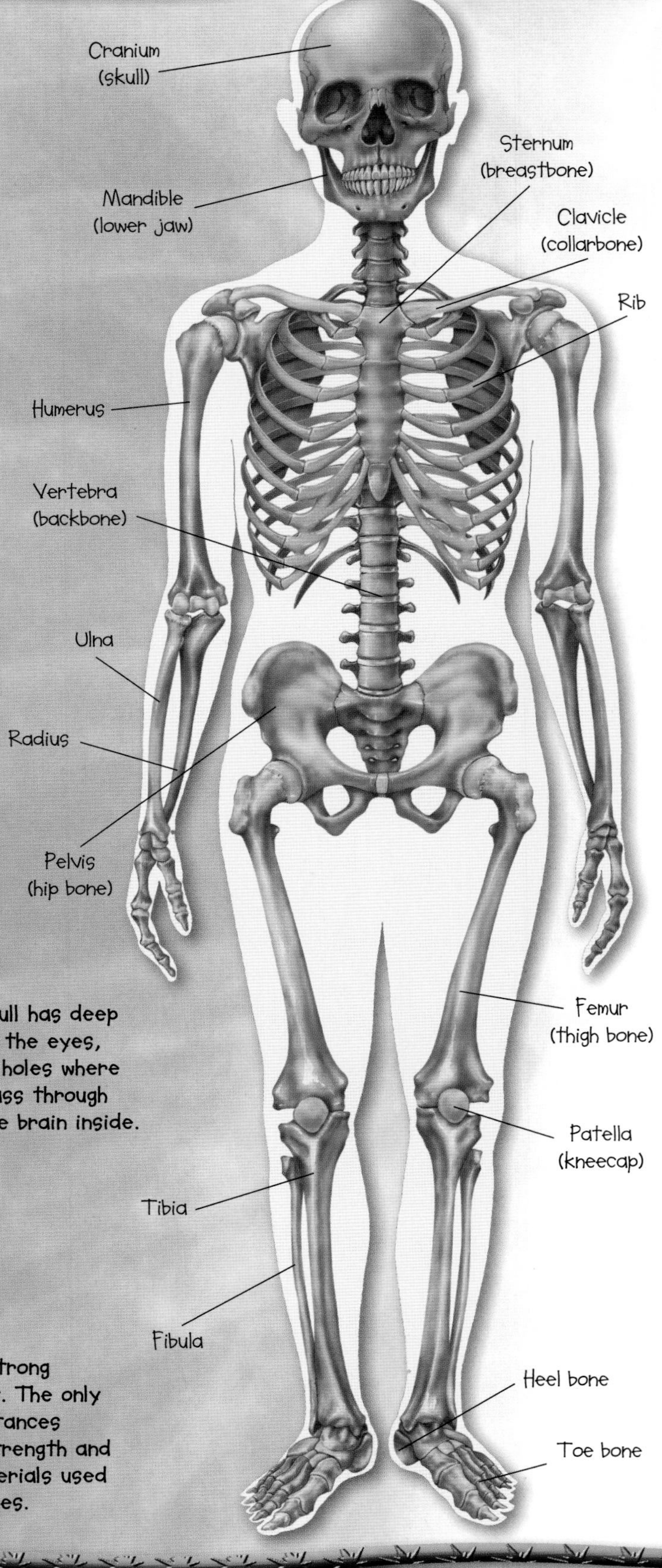

► The skeleton forms a strong framework inside the body. The only artificial (man-made) substances that can match bone for strength and lightness are some of the materials used to make racing cars and jet planes.

225
All the bones together make up the skeleton. Most people have 206 bones, from head to toe as follows:
• 8 in the upper part of the skull, the cranium or braincase
• 14 in the face
• 6 tiny ear bones, 3 deep in each ear
• 1 in the neck, which is floating and not directly connected to any other bone
• 26 in the spinal column or backbone
• 25 in the chest, being 24 ribs and the breastbone
• 32 in each arm, from shoulder to fingertips (8 in each wrist)
• 31 in each leg, from hip to toetips (7 in each ankle)

226
Bone contains threads of the tough, slightly bendy substance called collagen. It also has hard minerals such as calcium and phosphate. Together, the collagen and minerals make a bone strong and rigid, yet able to bend slightly under stress. Bones have blood vessels for nourishment and nerves to feel pressure and pain. Also, some bones are not solid. They contain a jelly-like substance called marrow. This makes tiny parts for the blood, called red and white blood cells.

Spongy bone

Marrow

Nerves and blood vessels

Compact (hard) bone

'Skin' of bone (periosteum)

End or head of bone

▲ Bone has a hard layer outside, a spongy layer next, and soft marrow in the middle.

NAME THE BONE!
Every bone has a scientific or medical name, and many have ordinary names too. Can you match up these ordinary and scientific names for various bones?

1. Mandible 2. Femur 3. Clavicle
4. Pelvis 5. Patella 6. Sternum

a. Thigh bone b. Breastbone
c. Kneecap d. Hip bone
e. Collarbone f. Lower jaw bone

Answers:
1f 2a 3e 4d 5c 6b

95

The flexible body

227 Without joints, almost the only parts of your body that could move would be your tongue and eyebrows! Joints between bones allow the skeleton to bend. You have more than 200 joints. The largest are in the hips and knees. The smallest are in the fingers, toes, and between the tiny bones inside each ear which help you hear.

228 There are several kinds of joints, depending on the shapes of the bone ends, and how much the bones can move. Bend your knee and your lower leg moves forwards and backwards, but not sideways. This is a hinge-type joint. Bend your hip and your leg can move forwards, backwards, and also from side to side. This is a ball-and-socket joint.

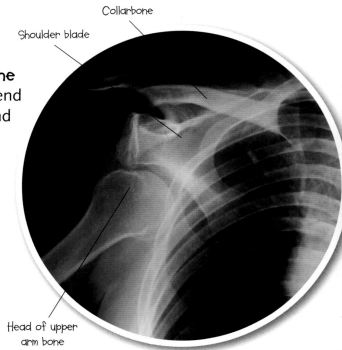

Collarbone

Shoulder blade

Head of upper arm bone

▶ This X-ray shows a dislocated (out of place) shoulder. The shoulder joint has the biggest range of movement, so this injury is common.

TEST YOUR JOINTS

Try using these different joints carefully, and see how much movement they allow. Can you guess the type of joint used in each one – hinge or ball-and-socket?

1. Fingertip joint (smallest knuckle)

2. Elbow

3. Hip

4. Shoulder

Answers:
1. hinge 2. hinge
3. ball-and-socket 4. ball-and-socket

229 Inside a joint where the bones come together, each bone end is covered with a smooth, shiny, slippery, slightly springy substance, known as cartilage. This is smeared with a thick liquid called synovial fluid. The fluid works like the oil in a car, to smooth the movements and reduce rubbing and wear between the cartilage surfaces.

230 The bones in a joint are linked together by a bag-like part, the capsule, and strong, stretchy, strap-like ligaments. The ligaments let the bones move but stop them coming apart or moving too far. The shoulder has seven strong ligaments.

231 In some joints, there are cartilage coverings over the bone ends and also pads of cartilage between the cartilage! These extra pads are called articular discs. There is one in each joint in the backbone, between the spinal bones, which are called vertebrae. There are also two of these extra cartilages, known as menisci, in each knee joint. They help the knee to 'lock' straight so that we can stand up without too much effort.

Muscle

Femur

Patella (kneecap)

Tendon

Ligament

Cartilage pad

Fibula

Tibia

▲ The knee has many ligaments, cartilage pads (menisci) and strong tendons that anchor muscles.

KEY
① Swivel joint
② Ellipsoidal joints
③ Saddle joint
④ Ball-and-socket joint
⑤ Hinge joint
⑥ Plane joints

◄ Synovial joints allow the body to move in many ways so we can walk, run, play and work.

When muscles pull

232 Almost half the body's weight is muscles, and there are more than 640 of them! Muscles have one simple but important job, which is to get shorter, or contract. A muscle cannot forcefully get longer.

▼ A tendon is stuck firmly into the bone it pulls, with a joint stronger than superglue!

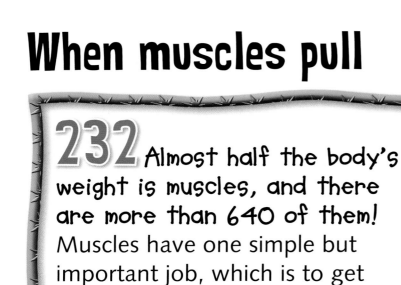

Tendon

Bone

Pectoralis

Biceps

Deltoid

Abdominal wall muscles

Trapezius

Rectus femoris

Gluteus

Semitendinosus

Gastrocnemius

▲ The muscles shown here are those just beneath the skin, called superficial muscles. Under them is another layer, the deep muscle layer. In some areas there is an additional layer, the medial muscles.

233 A muscle is joined to a bone by its tendon. This is where the end of the muscle becomes slimmer or tapers, and is strengthened by strong, thick fibres of collagen. The fibres are fixed firmly into the surface of the bone.

234 Some muscles are wide or broad, and shaped more like flat sheets or triangles. These include the three layers of muscles in the lower front and sides of the body, called the abdominal wall muscles. If you tense or contract them, they pull your tummy in to make you look thinner.

235
Most muscles are long and slim, and joined to bones at each end. As they contract they pull on the bones and move them. As this happens, the muscle becomes wider, or more bulging in the middle. To move the bone back again, a muscle on the other side of it contracts, while the first muscle relaxes and is pulled longer.

I DON'T BELIEVE IT!
It's easier to smile than to frown. There are about 40 muscles under the skin of the face. You use almost all of these to make a deep frown, but only about half of them to show a broad grin.

236
Every muscle in the body has a scientific or medical name, which is often quite long and complicated. Some of these names are familiar to people who do exercise and sports. The 'pecs' are the pectoralis major muscles across the chest. The 'biceps' are the biceps brachii muscles in the upper arms, which bulge when you bend your elbow.

▶ A breakdancer needs endurance, strength and control over their muscles to carry out moves such as this.

237
If you take plenty of exercise or play sport, you do not gain new muscles. But the muscles you have become larger and stronger. This keeps them fit and healthy. Muscles that are not used much may become weak and floppy.

▶ Muscles work in two-way pairs, like the biceps and triceps, which bend and straighten the elbow.

Biceps

Triceps

Biceps gets shorter and bends the elbow

To move the forearm back down, the triceps shortens and the biceps gets longer

Muscle power

238 **Muscles have many shapes and sizes, but inside they are all similar.** They have bundles of long, hair-like threads called muscle fibres, or myofibres. Each muscle fibre is slightly thinner than a hair. A big muscle has many thousands of them. Most are about 3 or 4 centimetres long. In a big muscle, many fibres of different lengths lie alongside each other and end-to-end.

Muscle fibre

Nerve branches

Muscle fibre

Muscle fibril

▶ Male gymnasts need extreme upper body strength when using the rings. Many different muscles work together to hold the gymnast in the correct position.

239 **Each muscle fibre is made of dozens or hundreds of even thinner parts, called muscle fibrils or myofibrils.** There are millions of these in a large muscle. And, as you may guess, each fibril contains hundreds of yet thinner threads! There are two kinds, actin and myosin. As the actins slide past and between the myosins, the threads get shorter – and the muscle contracts.

Body of muscle

◀ The main part of a muscle is the body or belly, with hundreds of muscle fibres inside.

Actin

Myosin

▶ Dozens of arm and hand muscles move a pen precisely, a tiny amount each time.

240
Muscles are controlled by the brain, which sends messages to them along string-like nerves. When a muscle contracts for a long time, its fibres 'take turns'. Some of them shorten powerfully while others relax, then the contracted ones relax while others shorten, and so on.

WHICH MUSCLES?

Can you match the names of these muscles with different parts of the body?

a. Gluteus maximus b. Masseter
c. Sartorius d. Cardiac muscle
e. Pectoralis major

1. Heart 2. Chest 3. Front of thigh
4. Buttock 5. Mouth

Answers:
a4 b5 c3 d1 e2

241
The body's biggest muscles are the ones you sit on – the gluteus maximus muscles in the buttocks. The longest muscle is the sartorius, across the front of the thigh. Some of its fibres are more than 30 centimetres in length. The most powerful muscle, for its size, is the masseter in the lower cheek, which closes the jaws when you chew.

The breathing body

242 **The body cannot survive more than a few minutes without breathing.** This action is so important, we do it all the time without thinking. We breathe to take air into the body. Air contains the gas oxygen, which is needed to get energy from food to power all of the body's vital life processes.

► Body parts make up the respiratory system in the head, neck and chest. These carry out the process of breathing air to take oxygen into the body.

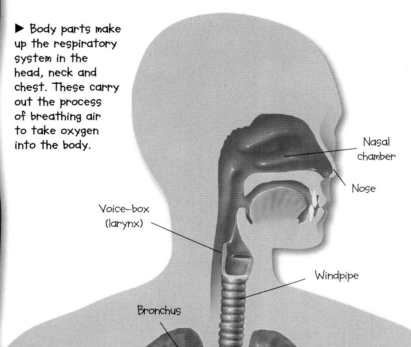

Nasal chamber

Nose

Voice-box (larynx)

Windpipe

Bronchus

Left lung

Diaphragm

▲ Scuba divers wear special breathing apparatus called 'aqua lungs'. They control their breathing to make their oxygen supply last as long as possible.

243 **Parts of the body that work together to carry out a main task are called a system.** The parts that carry out breathing are the respiratory system. These parts are the nose, throat, windpipe, the air tubes or bronchi in the chest, and the lungs.

244

The nose is the entrance for fresh air to the lungs – and the exit for stale air from the lungs. The soft, moist lining inside the nose makes air warmer and damper, which is better for the lungs. Tiny bits of floating dust and germs stick to the lining or the hairs in the nose, making the air cleaner.

▼ When playing the trumpet, the diaphragm and chest control the air flowing in and out of the lungs.

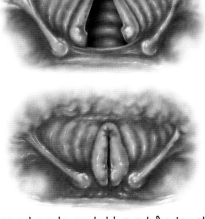

245

The windpipe, or trachea, is a tube leading from the back of the nose and mouth, down to the lungs. It has about 20 C-shaped hoops of cartilage in its wall to keep it open, like a vacuum cleaner hose. Otherwise the pressure of body parts in the neck and chest would squash it shut.

246

At the top of the windpipe, making a bulge at the front of the neck, is the voice box or larynx. It has two stiff flaps, vocal cords, which stick out from its sides. Normally these flaps are apart for easy breathing. But muscles in the voice-box can pull the flaps almost together. As air passes through the narrow slit between them it makes the flaps shake or vibrate – and this is the sound of your voice.

HUMMMMMM!

You will need:
stopwatch

Do you think making sounds with your voice box uses more air than breathing? Find out by following this experiment.

1. Take a deep breath in, then breathe out at your normal rate, for as long as you can. Time the out-breath.

2. Take a similar deep breath in, then hum as you breathe out, again for as long as you can. Time the hum.

3. Try the same while whispering your favourite song, then again when singing.

▲ The vocal cords are held apart for breathing (top) and pulled together for speech (bottom).

Breathing parts

247 The main parts of the respiratory (breathing) system are the two lungs in the chest. Each one is shaped like a tall cone, with the pointed end at shoulder level.

248 Air comes in and out of the lungs along the windpipe, which branches at its base to form two main air tubes, the bronchi. One goes to each lung. Inside the lung, each bronchus divides again and again, becoming narrower each time. Finally the air tubes, thinner than hairs, end at groups of tiny 'bubbles' called alveoli.

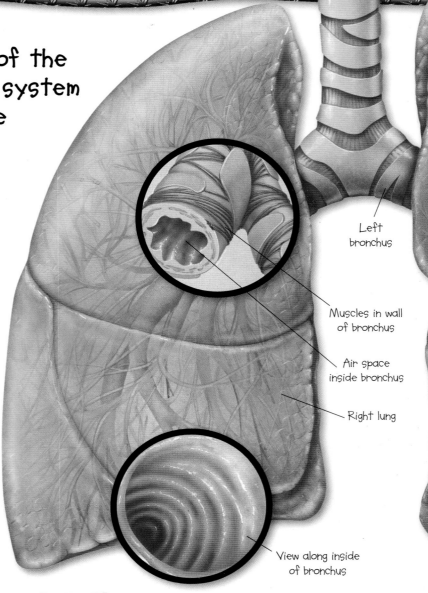

Left bronchus

Muscles in wall of bronchus

Air space inside bronchus

Right lung

View along inside of bronchus

I DON'T BELIEVE IT!

On average, the air breathed in and out through the night by a sleeping person, would fill an average-sized bedroom. This is why some people like to sleep with the door or window open!

249 There are more than 200 million tiny air bubbles, or alveoli, in each lung. Inside, oxygen from breathed-in air passes through the very thin linings of the alveoli to equally tiny blood vessels on the other side. The blood carries the oxygen away, around the body. At the same time a waste substance, carbon dioxide, seeps through the blood vessel, into the alveoli. As you breathe out, the lungs blow out the carbon dioxide.

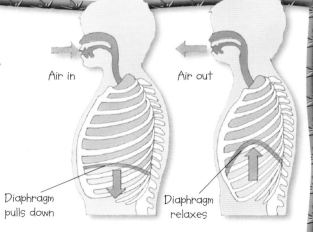

250
Breathing needs muscle power! The main breathing muscle is the dome-shaped diaphragm at the base of the chest. To breathe in, it becomes flatter, making the lungs bigger, so they suck in air down the windpipe. At the same time, rib muscles lift the ribs, also making the lungs bigger. To breathe out, the diaphragm and rib muscles relax. The stretched lungs spring back to their smaller size and blow out stale air.

▲ Breathing uses two main sets of muscles, the diaphragm and those between the ribs.

▶ After great activity, the body breathes faster and deeper, to replace the oxygen used by the muscles for energy.

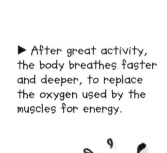

Bronchiole

Blood vessel

Air space in alveoli

Alveoli

▲ Inside each lung, the main bronchus divides again and again, into thousands of narrower airways called bronchioles.

251
As you rest or sleep, each breath sends about half a litre of air in and out, 15 to 20 times each minute. After great activity, such as running a race, you need more oxygen. So you take deeper breaths faster – 3 litres or more of air, 50 times or more each minute.

The hungry body

252 All machines need fuel to make them go, and the body is like a living machine whose fuel is food. Food gives us energy for our body processes inside, and for breathing, moving, talking and every other action we make. Food also provides raw materials that the body uses to grow, maintain itself and repair daily wear-and-tear.

253 We would not put the wrong fuel into a car engine, so we should not put unsuitable foods into the body. A healthy diet needs a wide variety of foods, which have lots of vital nutrients. Too much of one single food may be unhealthy, especially if that food is very fatty or greasy. Too much of all foods is also unhealthy, making the body overweight and increasing the risk of illnesses.

▶ It is important for children to learn how to cook healthily. Grilling or barbecuing food is much healthier than frying it.

▲ Fresh fruits such as bananas, and vegetables such as carrots, have lots of vitamins, minerals and fibre, and are good for the body in lots of ways.

▼ Foods such as bread, pasta and rice contain lots of starch, which is a useful energy source.

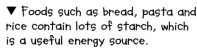

254 There are six main kinds of nutrients in foods, and the body needs balanced amounts of all of them.

- Proteins are needed for growth and repair, and for strong muscles and other parts.
- Carbohydrates, such as sugars and starches, give plenty of energy.
- Some fats are important for general health and energy.
- Vitamins help the body to fight germs and disease.
- Minerals are needed for strong bones and teeth and also healthy blood.
- Fibre is important for good digestion and to prevent certain bowel disorders.

◄ Fish, low-fat meats such as chicken, and dairy produce such as cheese all contain plenty of valuable proteins.

▲ Fats and oily foods are needed in moderate amounts. Plant oils are healthier than fats and oils from animal sources.

FOOD FOR THOUGHT

Which of these meals do you think is healthier?

Meal A
Burger, sausage and lots of chips, followed by ice cream with cream and chocolate.

Meal B
Chicken, tomato and a few chips, followed by fresh fruit salad with apple, banana, pear and melon.

Answer:
Meal B

Bite, chew, gulp

255 The hardest parts of your whole body are the ones that make holes in your food – teeth. They have a covering of whitish or yellowish enamel, which is stronger than most kinds of rocks! Teeth need to last a lifetime of biting, nibbling, gnashing, munching and chewing. They are your own food processors.

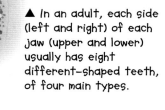

Incisor

Canine

Premolar

Molar

256 There are four main shapes of teeth. The front ones are incisors, and each has a straight, sharp edge, like a spade or chisel, to cut through food. Next are canines, which are taller and more pointed, used mainly for tearing and pulling. Behind them are premolars and molars, which are lower and flatter with small bumps, for crushing and grinding.

Jaw bone

Root

▲ In an adult, each side (left and right) of each jaw (upper and lower) usually has eight different-shaped teeth, of four main types.

▶ At the centre of a tooth is living pulp, with many blood vessels and nerve endings that pass into the jaw bone.

257 A tooth may look almost dead, but it is very much alive. Under the enamel is slightly softer dentine. In the middle of the tooth is the dental pulp. This has blood vessels to nourish the whole tooth, and nerves that feel pressure, heat, cold and pain. The lower part of the tooth, strongly fixed in the jaw bone, is the root. The enamel-covered part above the gum is the crown.

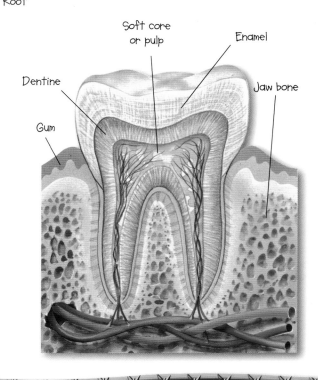

Soft core or pulp

Enamel

Dentine

Jaw bone

Gum

258

Teeth are very strong and tough, but they do need to be cleaned properly and regularly. Germs called bacteria live on old bits of food in the mouth. They make waste products which are acid and eat into the enamel and dentine, causing holes called cavities. Which do you prefer – cleaning your teeth after main meals and before bedtime, or the agony of toothache?

▶ Clean your teeth by brushing in different directions and then flossing between them. They will look better and stay healthier for longer.

▼ The first set of teeth lasts about ten years, while the second set can last ten times longer.

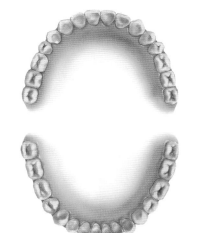

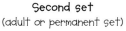

First set
(milk or deciduous teeth)

Second set
(adult or permanent set)

259

Teeth are designed to last a lifetime. Well, not quite, because the body has two sets. There are 20 small teeth in the first or baby set. The first ones usually appear above the gum by about six months of age, the last ones at three years old. As you and your mouth grow, the baby teeth fall out from about seven years old. They are replaced by 32 larger teeth in the adult set.

260

After chewing, food is swallowed into the gullet (oesophagus). This pushes the food powerfully down through the chest, past the heart and lungs, into the stomach.

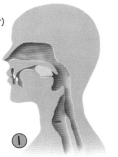

① Tongue pushes food to the back of the throat

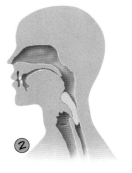

② Throat muscles squeeze the food downwards

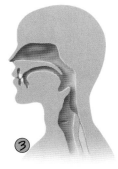

③ The oesophagus pushes food to the stomach

Food's long journey

261 The digestive system is like a tunnel about 9 metres long, through the body. It includes parts of the body that bite food, chew it, swallow it, churn it up and break it down with natural juices and acids, take in its goodness, and then get rid of the leftovers.

262 The stomach is a bag with strong, muscular walls. It stretches as it fills with food and drink, and its lining makes powerful digestive acids and juices called enzymes, to attack the food. The muscles in its walls squirm and squeeze to mix the food and juices.

263 The stomach digests food for a few hours into a thick mush, which oozes into the small intestine. This is only 4 centimetres wide, but more than 5 metres long. It takes nutrients and useful substances through its lining, into the body.

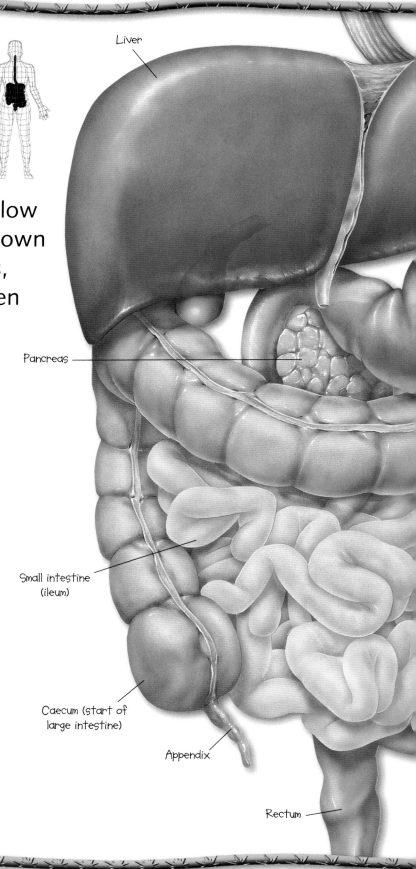

Liver

Pancreas

Small intestine (ileum)

Caecum (start of large intestine)

Appendix

Rectum

264

The large intestine follows the small one, and it is certainly wider, at about 6 centimetres, but much shorter, only 1.5 metres. It takes in fluids and a few more nutrients from the food, and then squashes what's left into brown lumps, ready to leave the body.

Stomach

Large intestine

Villus

Vessels inside villus

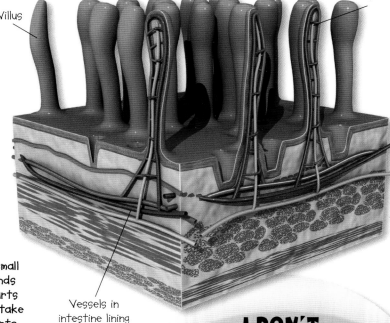

Vessels in intestine lining

▶ The lining of the small intestine has thousands of tiny finger-like parts called the villi, which take nutrients from food, into the blood and lymph system.

◀ The digestive parts almost fill the lower part of the main body, called the abdomen.

265

The liver and pancreas are also parts of the digestive system. The liver sorts out and changes the many nutrients from digestion, and stores some of them. The pancreas makes powerful digestive juices that pass to the small intestine to work on the food there.

I DON'T BELIEVE IT!

What's in the leftovers? The brown lumps called bowel motions or faeces are only about one-half undigested or leftover food. Some of the rest is rubbed-off parts of the stomach and intestine lining. The rest is millions of 'friendly' but dead microbes (bacteria) from the intestine. They help to digest our food for us, and in return we give them a warm, food-filled place to live.

Blood in the body

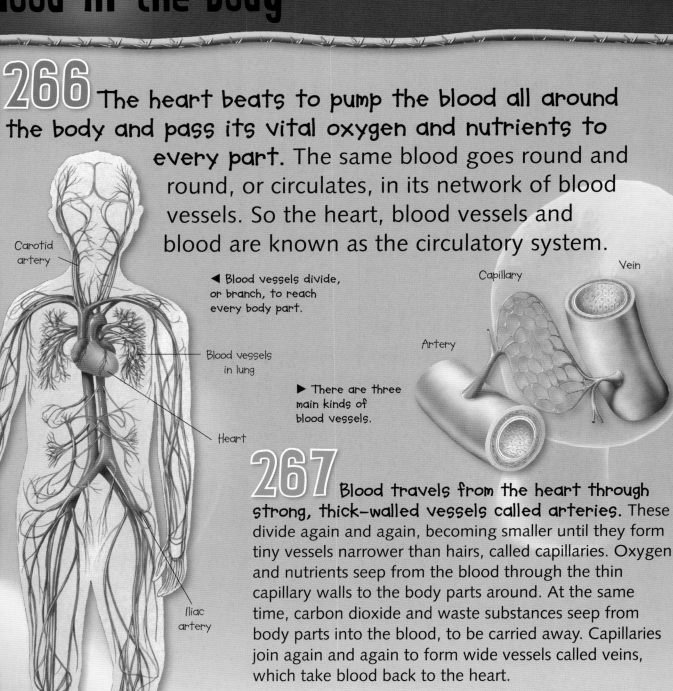

266 The heart beats to pump the blood all around the body and pass its vital oxygen and nutrients to every part. The same blood goes round and round, or circulates, in its network of blood vessels. So the heart, blood vessels and blood are known as the circulatory system.

Carotid artery

◀ Blood vessels divide, or branch, to reach every body part.

Blood vessels in lung

▶ There are three main kinds of blood vessels.

Heart

Capillary

Vein

Artery

Iliac artery

267 Blood travels from the heart through strong, thick-walled vessels called arteries. These divide again and again, becoming smaller until they form tiny vessels narrower than hairs, called capillaries. Oxygen and nutrients seep from the blood through the thin capillary walls to the body parts around. At the same time, carbon dioxide and waste substances seep from body parts into the blood, to be carried away. Capillaries join again and again to form wide vessels called veins, which take blood back to the heart.

268 In addition to delivering oxygen and nutrients, and carrying away carbon dioxide and wastes, blood has many other vital tasks. It carries body control substances called hormones. It spreads heat evenly around the body from busy, warmer parts such as the heart, liver and muscles. It forms a sticky clot to seal a cut. It carries many substances that attack germs and other tiny invaders.

269 Blood has four main parts. The largest is billions of tiny, saucer-shaped red cells, which make up almost half of the total volume of blood and carry oxygen. Second is the white cells, which clean the blood, prevent disease and fight germs. The third part is billions of tiny platelets, which help blood to clot. Fourth is watery plasma, in which the other parts float.

QUIZ
Can you match these blood parts and vessels with their descriptions?
a. Artery b. Vein c. White blood cell
d. Red blood cell e. Platelet f. Capillary

1. Large vessel that takes blood back to the heart
2. Tiny vessel allowing oxygen and nutrients to leave blood
3. Large vessel carrying blood away from the heart
4. Oxygen–carrying part of the blood
5. Disease–fighting part of the blood
6. Part that helps blood to clot

Answers: a3 b1 c5 d4 e6 f2

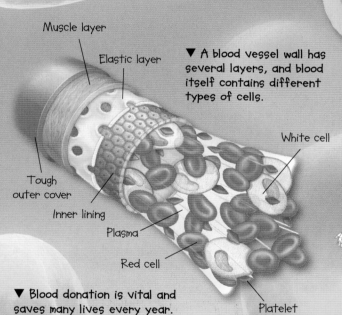

Muscle layer
Elastic layer
▼ A blood vessel wall has several layers, and blood itself contains different types of cells.
White cell
Tough outer cover
Inner lining
Plasma
Red cell
Platelet

▼ Blood donation is vital and saves many lives every year.

A Positive

► Each kidney has about one million tiny filters, called nephrons, in its outer layer, or cortex.

Cortex Medulla
Blood vessels
Ureter

270 Blood is cleaned by two kidneys, situated in the middle of your back. They filter the blood and make a liquid called urine, which contains unwanted and waste substances, plus excess or 'spare' water. The urine trickles from each kidney down a tube, the ureter, into a stretchy bag, the bladder. It's stored here until you can get rid of it – at your convenience.

The beating body

271 **The heart is about as big as its owner's clenched fist.** It is a hollow bag of very strong muscle, called cardiac muscle or myocardium. This muscle never tires. It contracts once every second or more often, all through life. The contraction, or heartbeat, squeezes blood inside the heart out into the arteries. As the heart relaxes it fills again with blood from the veins.

272 **Inside, the heart is not one bag-like pump, but two pumps side by side.** The left pump sends blood all around the body, from head to toe, to deliver its oxygen (systemic circulation). The blood comes back to the right pump and is sent to the lungs, to collect more oxygen (pulmonary circulation). The blood returns to the left pump and starts the whole journey again.

▶ The heart is two pumps side by side, and each pump has two chambers, the upper atrium and the lower ventricle.

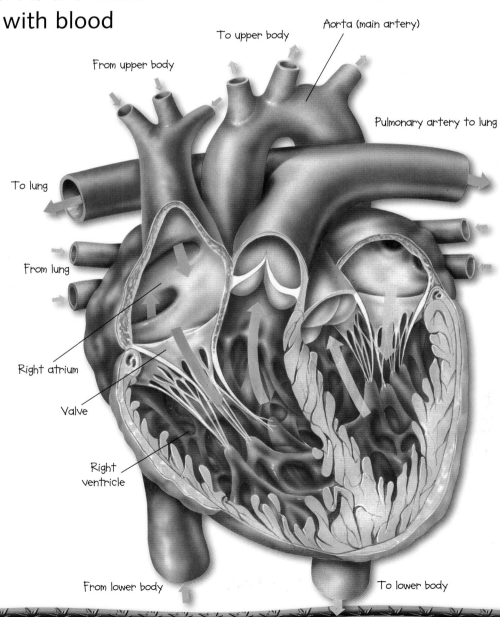

To upper body

Aorta (main artery)

From upper body

Pulmonary artery to lung

To lung

From lung

Right atrium

Valve

Right ventricle

From lower body

To lower body

273
Inside the heart are four sets of bendy flaps called valves. These open to let blood flow the right way. If the blood tries to move the wrong way, it pushes the flaps together and the valve closes. Valves make sure the blood flows the correct way, rather than sloshing to and fro, in and out of the heart, with each beat.

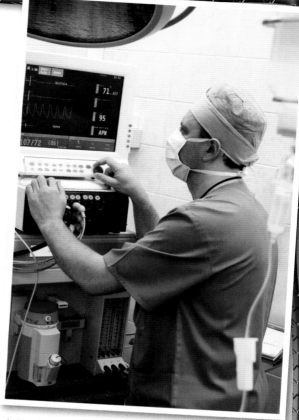

▲ Doctors use ECG machines to monitor the electrical activity of the heart.

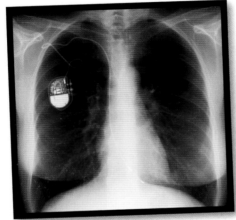

► This X-ray of a chest shows a pacemaker that has been implanted to control an irregular heartbeat.

274
The heart is the body's most active part, and it needs plenty of energy brought by the blood. The blood flows through small vessels, which branch across its surface and down into its thick walls. These are called the coronary vessels.

275
The heart beats at different rates, depending on what the body is doing. When the muscles are active they need more energy and oxygen, brought by the blood. So the heart beats faster, 120 times each minute or more. At rest, the heart slows to 60 to 80 beats per minute.

HOW FAST IS YOUR HEARTBEAT?
You will need:
plastic funnel   tracing paper
plastic tube (like hosepipe)   sticky-tape

You can hear your heart and count its beats with a sound-funnel device called a stethoscope.

1. Stretch the tracing paper over the funnel's wide end and tape in place. Push a short length of tube over the funnel's narrow end.

2. Place the funnel's wide end over your heart, on your chest, just to the left, and put the tube end to your ear. Listen to and count your heartbeat.

Looking and listening

276 The body finds out about the world around it by its senses — and the main sense is eyesight. The eyes detect the brightness, colours and patterns of light rays, and change these into patterns of nerve signals that they send to the brain. More than half of the knowledge, information and memories stored in the brain come into the body through the eyes.

▶ The eye is moved by six tiny muscles, and inside, it is filled with a clear fluid, vitreous humour.

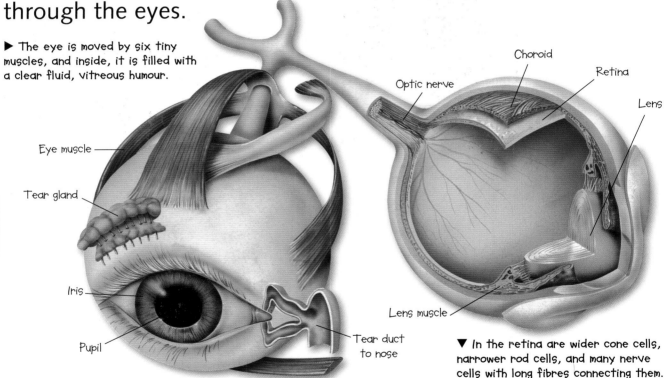

Eye muscle

Tear gland

Iris

Pupil

Tear duct to nose

Optic nerve

Choroid

Retina

Lens

Lens muscle

277 Each eye is a ball about 2.5 centimetres across. At the front is a clear dome, the cornea, which lets light through a small, dark-looking hole just behind it, the pupil. The light then passes through a pea-shaped lens, which bends the rays so they shine a clear picture onto the inside back of the eye, the retina. This has 125 million tiny cells, rods and cones, which detect the light and make nerve signals to send along the optic nerve to the brain.

▼ In the retina are wider cone cells, narrower rod cells, and many nerve cells with long fibres connecting them.

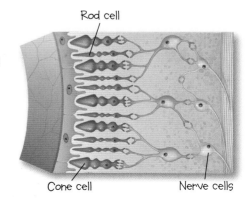

Rod cell

Cone cell

Nerve cells

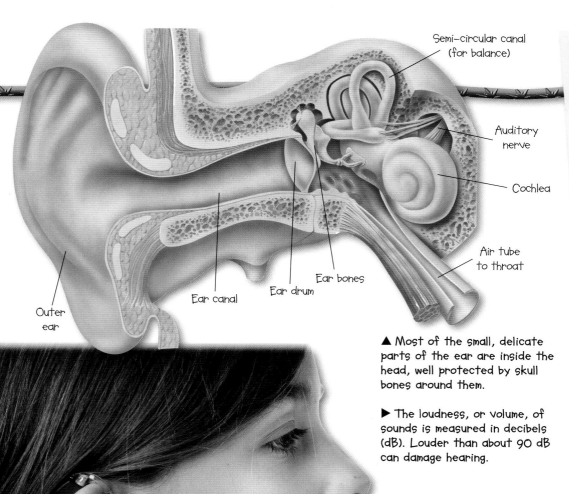

Semi-circular canal
(for balance)

Auditory
nerve

Cochlea

Air tube
to throat

Ear bones

Ear drum

Ear canal

Outer
ear

▲ Most of the small, delicate parts of the ear are inside the head, well protected by skull bones around them.

▶ The loudness, or volume, of sounds is measured in decibels (dB). Louder than about 90 dB can damage hearing.

Atom bomb 210 dB

Jet take-off 140 dB

Thunder 100 dB

Talking 40 dB

Rustling leaves 10 dB

◀ Some people need help to hear properly. A hearing aid worn inside the ear can help them to hear better.

BRIGHT AND DIM

Look at your eyes in a mirror. See how the dark hole which lets in light, the pupil, is quite small. The coloured part around the pupil, the iris, is a ring of muscle.

Close your eyes for a minute, then open them and look carefully. Does the pupil quickly get smaller?

While the eyes were closed, the iris made the pupil bigger, to try and let in more light, so you could try to see in the darkness. As you open your eyes, the iris makes the pupil smaller again, to prevent too much light from dazzling you.

278 The ear flap funnels sound waves along a short tunnel, the ear canal to the eardrum. As sound waves hit the eardrum it shakes or vibrates, and passes the vibrations to a row of three tiny bones. These are the ear ossicles, the smallest bones in the body. They also vibrate and pass on the vibrations to another part, the cochlea.

279 Inside the cochlea, the vibrations pass through fluid and shake rows of thousands of tiny hairs that grow from specialized hair cells. As the hairs vibrate, the hair cells make nerve signals, which flash along the auditory nerve to the brain.

Smelling and tasting

▼ The parts that carry out smelling are in the roof of the large chamber inside the nose.

Olfactory cells

Nasal cavity

Mucus lining

280 You cannot see smells, which are tiny particles floating in the air – but your nose can smell them. Your nose can detect more than 10,000 different scents, odours and fragrances. Smell is useful because it warns us if food is bad or rotten, and perhaps dangerous to eat. That's why we sniff a new or strange food item before trying it.

281 Smell particles drift with breathed-in air into the nose and through the nasal chamber behind it. At the top of the chamber are two patches of lining, each about the area of a thumbnail and with 5 million olfactory cells. The particles land on their sticky hairs, and if they fit into landing sites called receptors there, like a key into a lock, then nerve signals flash along the olfactory nerve to the brain.

▶ Olfactory (smell) cells have micro-hairs facing down into the nasal chamber, which detect smell particles landing on them.

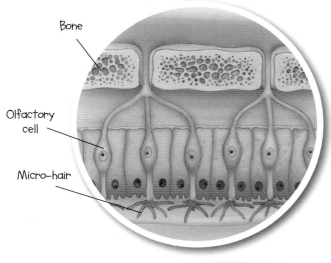

Bone

Olfactory cell

Micro-hair

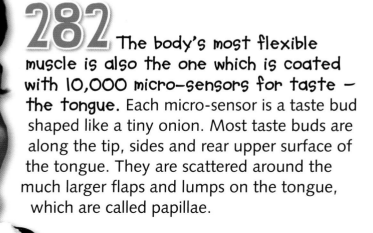

282
The body's most flexible muscle is also the one which is coated with 10,000 micro-sensors for taste — the tongue. Each micro-sensor is a taste bud shaped like a tiny onion. Most taste buds are along the tip, sides and rear upper surface of the tongue. They are scattered around the much larger flaps and lumps on the tongue, which are called papillae.

◀ The tongue is sensitive to flavours, texture and temperature.

283
Taste works in a similar way to smell, but it detects flavour particles in foods and drinks. The particles touch tiny hairs sticking up from hair cells in the taste buds. If the particles fit into receptors there, then the hair cell makes nerve signals, which go along the facial and other nerves to the brain.

SWEET AND SOUR

The tongue detects at least five basic tastes.

Which of these foods is umami (savoury), sweet, salty, bitter or sour?

1. Coffee 2. Lemon 3. Bacon
4. Ice cream 5. Mushroom

Answers:
1. bitter 2. sour 3. salty
4. sweet 5. umami (savoury)

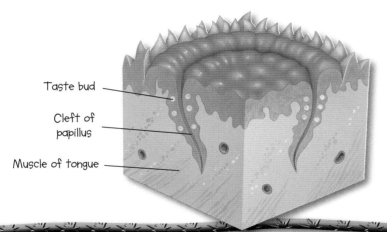

Taste bud

Cleft of papillus

Muscle of tongue

◀ The large pimple-like lumps at the back of the tongue, called papillae, have tiny taste buds in their deep clefts.

The nervous body

Brain

Spinal cord

Sciatic nerve

Tibial nerve

284
The body is not quite a 'bag of nerves', but it does contain thousands of kilometres of these pale, shiny threads. Nerves carry tiny electrical pulses known as nerve signals or neural messages. They form a vast information-sending network that reaches every part, almost like the body's own Internet.

285
Each nerve is a bundle of much thinner parts called nerve fibres. Like wires in a telephone cable, these carry their own tiny electrical nerve signals. A typical nerve signal has a strength of 0.1 volts (one-fifteenth as strong as a torch battery). The slowest nerve signals travel about half a metre each second, the fastest at more than 100 metres per second.

◀ Nerves branch from the brain and spinal cord to every body part.

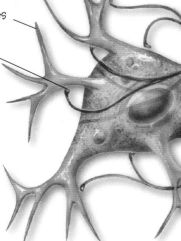

Axon

Dendrites

Synapse (junction between nerve cells)

286
All nerve signals are similar, but there are two main kinds, depending on where they are going. Sensory nerve signals travel from the sensory parts (eyes, ears, nose, tongue and skin) to the brain. Motor nerve signals travel from the brain out to the muscles, to make the body move about.

▶ The brain and nerves are made of billions of specialized cells, nerve cells or neurons. Each has many tiny branches, dendrites, to collect nerve messages, and a longer, thicker branch, the axon or fibre, to pass on the messages.

287 Hormones are part of the body's inner control system. A hormone is a chemical made by a gland. It travels in the blood and affects other body parts, for example, making them work faster or release more of their product.

288 The main hormonal gland, the pituitary, is also the smallest. Just under the brain, it has close links with the nervous system. It mainly controls other hormonal glands. One is the thyroid in the neck, which affects the body's growth and how fast its chemical processes work. The pancreas controls how the body uses energy by its hormone, insulin. The adrenal glands are involved in the body's balance of water, minerals and salts, and how we react to stress and fear.

▲ Sports such as snowboarding cause us to produce more adrenaline due to excitement and fear.

◄ Female and male bodies have much the same hormone-making glands, except for the reproductive parts – ovaries in the female (left) and testes in the male (right).

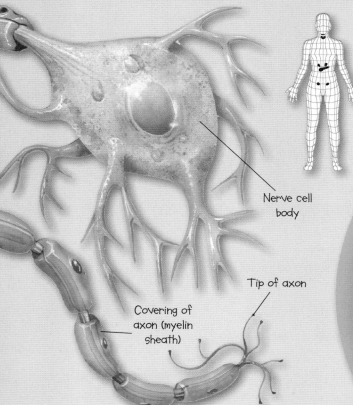

Nerve cell body

Tip of axon

Covering of axon (myelin sheath)

TIME TO REACT!

You will need:
friend ruler

1. Ask a friend to hold a ruler by the highest measurement so it hangs down. Put your thumb and fingers level with the other end, ready to grab.
2. When your friend lets go grasp it and measure where your thumb is on the ruler. Swap places so your friend has a go.
3. The person who grabs the ruler nearest its lower end has the fastest reactions. To grab the ruler, nerve signals travel from the eye, to the brain, and back to the muscles in the arm and hand.

The brainy body

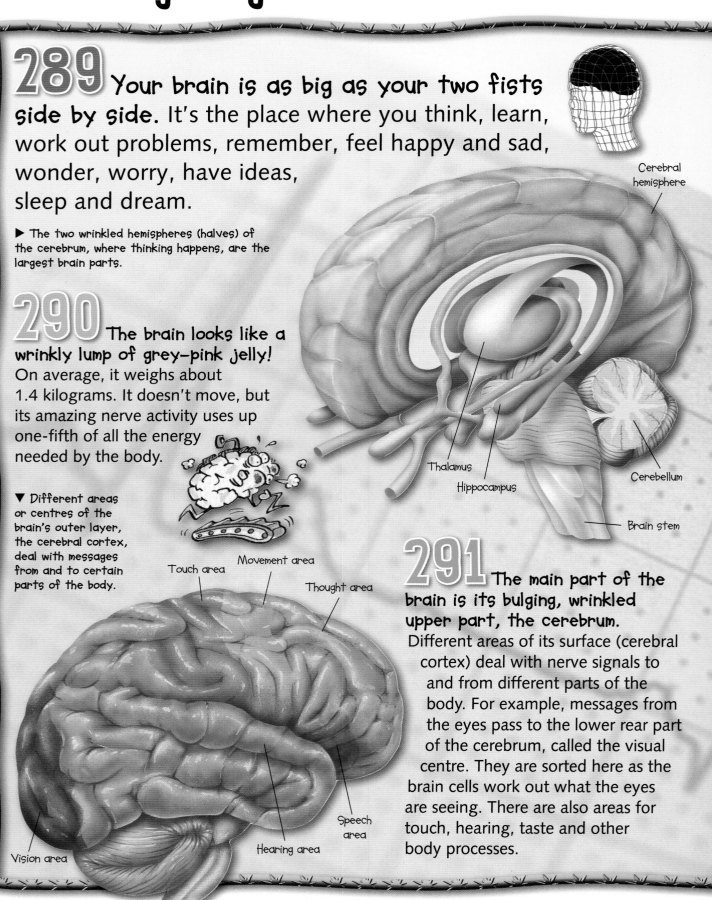

289 Your brain is as big as your two fists side by side. It's the place where you think, learn, work out problems, remember, feel happy and sad, wonder, worry, have ideas, sleep and dream.

▶ The two wrinkled hemispheres (halves) of the cerebrum, where thinking happens, are the largest brain parts.

290 The brain looks like a wrinkly lump of grey-pink jelly! On average, it weighs about 1.4 kilograms. It doesn't move, but its amazing nerve activity uses up one-fifth of all the energy needed by the body.

▼ Different areas or centres of the brain's outer layer, the cerebral cortex, deal with messages from and to certain parts of the body.

Cerebral hemisphere

Thalamus

Hippocampus

Cerebellum

Brain stem

Touch area

Movement area

Thought area

Vision area

Hearing area

Speech area

291 The main part of the brain is its bulging, wrinkled upper part, the cerebrum. Different areas of its surface (cerebral cortex) deal with nerve signals to and from different parts of the body. For example, messages from the eyes pass to the lower rear part of the cerebrum, called the visual centre. They are sorted here as the brain cells work out what the eyes are seeing. There are also areas for touch, hearing, taste and other body processes.

292
The cerebellum is the rounded, wrinkled part at the back of the brain. It processes messages from the motor centre, sorting and co-ordinating them in great detail, to send to the body's hundreds of muscles. This is how we learn skilled, precise movements such as writing, skateboarding or playing music (or all three), almost without thinking.

293
The brain stem is the lower part of the brain, where it joins the body's main nerve, the spinal cord. The brain stem controls basic processes vital for life, like breathing, heartbeat, digesting food and removing wastes.

▲ Our brains allow us to draw from memory, expressing emotions.

294
The brain really does have 'brain waves'. Every second it receives, sorts and sends millions of nerve signals. Special pads attached to the head can detect these tiny electrical pulses. They are shown on a screen or paper strip as wavy lines called an EEG, electro-encephalogram.

▼ The brain's 'waves' or EEG recordings change, depending on whether the person is alert and thinking hard, resting, falling asleep or deeply asleep.

I DON'T BELIEVE IT!
The brain never sleeps! EEG waves show that it is almost as busy at night as when we are awake. It still controls heartbeat, breathing and digestion. It also sifts through the day's events and stores memories.

The healthy body

295 No one wants to be ill – and it is very easy to cut down the risk of becoming sick or developing disease. For a start, the body needs the right amounts of different foods, especially fresh foods like vegetables and fruits. And not too much food either, or it becomes unhealthily fat.

296 Another excellent way to stay well is regular sport or exercise. Activity keeps the muscles powerful, the bones strong and the joints flexible. If it speeds up your breathing and heartbeat, it keeps your lungs and heart healthy too.

297 Germs are everywhere – in the air, on our bodies and on almost everything we touch. If we keep clean by showering or bathing, and especially if we wash our hands after using the toilet and before eating, then germs have less chance to attack us.

298 Health is not only in the body, it's in the mind. Too much worry and stress can cause many illnesses, such as headaches and digestive upsets. This is why it's so important to talk about troubles and share them with someone who can help.

▼ Germs on hands can get onto our food and then into our bodies. So it is important to wash hands before mealtimes.

299

Doctors and nurses help us to recover from sickness, and they also help prevent illness. Regular check-ups at the dentist, optician and health centre are vital. For most people immunizations (vaccinations) also help to protect against diseases. It is good to report any health problem early, before it becomes too serious to treat.

▼ In some immunizations, dead versions of a germ are put into the body using a syringe, so the body can develop resistance to them without suffering from the disease they cause.

300

Old age is getting older! More people live to be 100 years or more and for many of them, their bodies are still working well. How would you like to spend your 100th birthday?

▼ Exercise keeps the body fit and healthy, and it should be fun too. It is always best to reduce risks of having an accident by wearing a cycle helmet for example.

EVOLUTION

301
Earth is about 4600 million years old. At first our planet could not support life. It was a mass of red-hot, liquid rock often battered by meteorites (rocks from space). Over millions of years Earth cooled down and conditions changed, making it possible for life to exist. The first organisms (life forms) appeared on Earth about 3500 million years ago.

▼ We don't know for certain what Earth looked like more than 3000 million years ago before life began. There were many volcanoes, but no oceans.

302
The first organisms were very simple — just a single cell. Cells are the tiny, basic building blocks of all living things. Over millions of years life has become incredibly varied and complex, adapting to Earth's ever-changing environments. For example, the animal kingdom includes birds, insects, fish, reptiles and mammals. This amazing development is called 'evolution'.

303 Evolution has been studied for more than one hundred years. In the 18th century, scientists such as Charles Darwin (1809–1882) started forming theories to explain the vast changes in life over time. Since then, scientists have continued to examine living things and fossils – the remains of once-living organisms preserved in rocks – to explain how evolution works.

The riddle of life

304 A species is a type of living thing. All the individuals of a species have a similar appearance. They can breed with each other to produce offspring (babies). There are millions of different species alive today, as well as millions that have become extinct (died out completely).

305 Darwin was not the first scientist to write about evolution. French scientist Jean-Bapiste Lamarck (1744–1829) had a theory that if an animal adapted to its environment during its lifetime, the changes would be passed on to its offspring. Although not entirely correct, his ideas sparked interest. Other scientists also began to question whether God had created species as they now exist.

◄ Lamarck falsely believed that if a giraffe stretched its neck to reach the highest leaves on a tree, its neck would get longer — and its offspring would have longer necks too.

306 For centuries, people thought that a species could not change. Darwin examined mockingbirds from the Galápagos Islands and found differences between the specimens. He had an idea that the birds may have adapted to the islands' different environments. Darwin showed that a species could change over time and does not have a 'fixed' appearance.

► As Darwin explored the Galápagos Islands, he noticed small differences between the mockingbird species on each separate island.

▼ Each of these butterflies is a different species. They do not breed with each other and look different.

Brown argus

Purple emperor

Clouded yellow

Adonis blue

Green hairstreak

307 Each new individual inherits its genes from its parents (see page 80). The parental genes are shuffled so that the offspring has features from both parents. This creates variation, which is essential for evolution as it allows new features to develop. A clone is an individual that is genetically identical to another.

▲ All bananas from the same tree are clones of each other. They have the same DNA and so are genetically identical.

308 A mutation is a change within the DNA. If DNA is altered or damaged, its code is changed and a new form of the gene is created. Mutations are important as they can be inherited. If a species develops a useful characteristic, it will be passed on to its offspring.

309 A gene exists in different forms. Usually there is a dominant and a recessive form. For example, one gene controls hair length in cats. Long hair is dominant and short hair is recessive. To be short-haired, a cat needs to inherit a recessive gene from both parents.

▼ The female nine-banded armadillo usually has four offspring. They all come from one fertilized egg and so they are clones of each other.

▶ A recessive mutation produced this white tiger. White tigers cannot see as well as the normal orange tiger. As the mutation does not benefit the tiger, the gene is less likely to be passed on.

Classifying species

310 All living organisms are related and are linked in a huge web of life. To keep track of the vast number of species, living things can be classified (put into groups).

311 One method of classifying life is called cladistics. A clade is a group made up of an ancestor (a relative from the past) and all its living and extinct descendants, which developed from them. A clade is based on features that have been inherited, or passed on, from the ancestor. Usually, only the descendants have the specific feature.

COMMON ANCESTOR

Animals with stalks attached to the sea floor. Crinoids have cup-shaped bodies and many feathery arms

Crinoids

Moving animals with mouths on the underside of their bodies

Star-shaped body with central disc and radiating arms

Large central disc and four or more radiating arms

Starfish

Smaller central disc than starfish and snake-like arms

Brittlestars

Round body shape with no arms

Body covered in long spines

Sea urchins

Elongated body with leathery skin

Sea cucumbers

▲ ECHINODERM CLADE
Echinoderms are a unique group of animals, which have a spiny skin and five or more arms that radiate (branch) out from a body made up of five equal parts.

CLASSIFYING SHOES

You will need:
pen   notepad   lots of shoes

1. Divide the shoes into groups such as trainers, boots, wellies.

2. Separate each group into smaller groups, using features such as heels, laces and so on.

3. Keep dividing the groups until each shoe has its own group. Draw a chart to show how you classified the shoes.

312 All humans are related to the very first human beings. These first humans shared an ancestor with chimpanzees. If we look back further still, all primates – the animal group that includes monkeys and apes such as chimps and humans – share the same shrew-like, mammalian ancestor.

313

The scientist Carolus Linnaeus (1707–1778) classified organisms in a clear, scientific way. He arranged species into groups according to their body features and gave each species a unique Latin name. Each name is made up of two words, for example, the tiger is *Panthera tigris*.

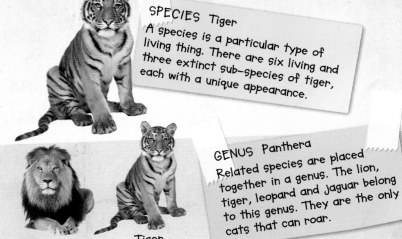

SPECIES Tiger
A species is a particular type of living thing. There are six living and three extinct sub-species of tiger, each with a unique appearance.

GENUS Panthera
Related species are placed together in a genus. The lion, tiger, leopard and jaguar belong to this genus. They are the only cats that can roar.

Lion   Tiger

FAMILY Felidae
The members of a family are closely related. There are 41 members of the felidae cat family.

Caracal   Domestic cat   Tiger   Cheetah

Red fox   Tiger   Sea lion   Wolf
Weasel

ORDER Carnivora
In an order, species are grouped together due to shared characteristics. Animals in the carnivora order are all meat-eating mammals.

CLASS Mammals
There are five vertebrate classes – birds, amphibians, reptiles, fish and mammals. All mammals have hair, breathe air and feed their young milk.

Bat   Whale   Gorilla   Tiger   Koala   Rabbit   Polar bear

314

Scientists used to classify different species purely by their appearance. For example plants were grouped according to leaf shape, or the colour and number of their petals. The study of DNA made scientists change their ideas about evolution and reclassify many species.

Frog   Sailfish
Hummingbird   Tiger   Crocodile

PHYLUM Chordates
Animals are grouped in different phylums depending on their body structure. Chordates have a spinal cord. Most are vertebrates (backboned animals).

Dragonfly   Toad   Snail   Eagle
Tiger
Starfish   Jellyfish   Shark   Snake   Crab

KINGDOM Animalia
All living things are placed into five main groups, including animals, plants and fungi.

The struggle for survival

315 Many things can affect an animal's survival. For example, food supply, disease and climate. If there is a change, some individuals may survive the new conditions. The survivors pass on their favourable genes to their young – this is natural selection.

◀ Predators such as polar bears target their hunts at weak or sick animals. The healthier, fitter animals tend to survive and reproduce.

316 Natural selection can cause changes within a species. The ancestors of modern tigers may have had fewer stripes. Stripes give good camouflage as they help the animal blend in with its surroundings. The ancestors with the gene for more stripes may have been the most successful hunters, and so would have raised more offspring, passing on the genes for stripy coats.

▼▶ These are three of the different ways animals have evolved to ensure their genes are passed on.

APPEARANCE
A camouflaged appearance gives this tiger a natural advantage while hunting.

SEXUAL SELECTION
Stags with the biggest antlers and best fighting technique are more likely to win females and have young.

LOTS OF OFFSPRING
Some animals, such as toads, have to have lots of young as many won't survive to adulthood.

317 When species change due to natural selection, evolution takes place. This process of selection has led to all the different species alive today. It is also one reason species can become extinct, as the least successful animals die out.

318

If a species is separated and isolated this too can cause evolution. When a group of individuals is cut off from others of the same species, they can only breed with each other. As they adapt to the new local conditions they evolve into a new species, unable to breed with the original group they were separated from.

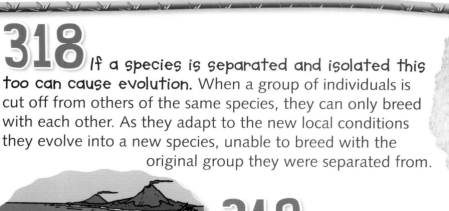

▼▶ The Galápagos Islands provided a range of environments to which the finches adapted.

SOUTH AMERICA

Galápagos Islands

319

A group of animals can be isolated by a river, an ocean or a mountain range. The Galápagos Islands are isolated from South America by the Pacific Ocean. Thousands of years ago, a few finches were blown there by strong winds. They stayed on the islands and bred, evolving separately from the mainland birds.

▼▶ There are about 14 different finch species on the Galápagos Islands. Each has a different beak shape suited to its particular diet.

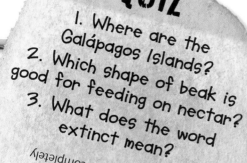

Common cactus finch

Beak Long and pointed
Diet Nectar of cactus flowers

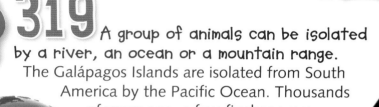

Large ground finch

Beak Large and thick
Diet Nuts, seeds and cactus fruits

Vegetarian tree finch

Beak Short, thick, parrot–like
Diet Plant buds, flowers, leaves

Woodpecker finch

Beak Pointed and narrow
Diet Insects and grubs

133

Looking for evidence

320 To show how species evolve, scientists look for evidence. They can examine and compare rocks, fossils and DNA (a substance inside most cells that carries all the genes for a living thing) for clues to back up their theories.

322 The study of rocks can tell us about the climate on Earth millions of years ago. Rocks that are rich in corals and the skeletons of other marine animals were formed when there were tropical oceans covering the land.

▼ Coelacanths (say 'seel-uh-kanths') were thought to be extinct until a living specimen was found in 1938. They are descended from the group of fish that evolved into amphibians.

Bony scales for protection not found on other live fish

Long, limb-like fins are used to 'walk' through the water

321 Fossils tell us what plants and animals looked like millions of years ago. Scientists compare living species with fossils of extinct species to see how much they have evolved over time.

323 Scientists can extract DNA from living cells to read their genetic code. The DNA of different organisms is compared to see how closely related they are. The most closely related have similar DNA.

◄ This fossil coelacanth shows that the fish has changed little over time.

Tenrecs are small, spiny animals found mostly in Madagascar. Their closest relatives are elephants and aardvarks

Prickly hedgehogs are found in Europe, Africa, parts of Asia and New Zealand

The echidna from Australia uses its long snout to find ants and termites

324 Some unrelated species have evolved similar traits.
Animals in different parts of the world have evolved spines for protection, while hummingbirds, butterflies and possums all have long tongues for probing into flowers to reach nectar. This is called convergent evolution.

▲ Tenrecs, hedgehogs and echidnas are unrelated species, yet they have each evolved similar body features because they live in similar environments.

325 Where animals are found in the world tells us about how they evolved.
When Madagascar became separated from Africa, lemurs (a type of primate) became isolated, and evolved separately from other African primates.

AFRICA

Madagascar

▲ Madagascar split from the coast of Africa about 165 million years ago.

▲ Lemurs, such as these ring-tailed lemurs, are found only in Madagascar.

135

Fossil clues

326 Fossils are the remains of living organisms that have been preserved in the ground. Most fossils are of animals, but plants can be fossilized too. The oldest fossils are of cyanobacteria (simple, single-celled organisms) that lived more than 3000 million years ago.

▼ The fossil magnolia (left) looks almost identical to the fruit from a living magnolia plant.

327 Fossil formation is a slow process. Some fossils can form in just 10,000 years, but most take much longer – usually hundreds of thousands, or even millions of years.

328 When an animal dies, its body might be buried under a layer of mud and sand. The soft body parts rot away but the hard parts, such as the bones, remain and become rock-like.

TRUE OR FALSE?

1. Fossils can be millions of years old.
2. The deeper the rock the younger the fossil.
3. Fossils helped Darwin work out his theory of evolution.

Answers:
1. True 2. False, usually the deeper the rock the older the fossil 3. True

▲ These palaeontologists (scientists who study the history of life on Earth) are working on an excavation or 'dig' in Wyoming in the United States, where dinosaur fossils have been found.

► These fossils were found in the La Brea Tar Pits near Los Angeles, United States. In the past, animals became trapped in the tar and died.

329 Scientists can learn how an extinct species lived by studying its fossil. For example, the structure and joints of an animal's legs shows how the animal walked, and how its muscles were attached to its skeleton.

AS WE COMPLETE EACH PIECE, WE FILL IT IN. KEEP CHECKING BACK TO WATCH OUR PROGRESS!

American lion (Panthera atrox) skeleton

■ Right Side Elements
■ Left Side Elements
■ Central Elements

330 The study of fossils helped Darwin work out his theory of evolution. He noticed that animal fossils found on islands such as the Cape Verde Islands and Falkland Islands in the Atlantic Ocean looked different from those he found on the South American mainland, giving him ideas about separation and isolation.

331 Fossils can be dated to find out when they lived on Earth. One way is to work out the age of the rock in which they were found. Usually, the deeper the rock, the older the fossil. To work out a fossil's absolute age, scientists make use of carbon-dating. All living things contain natural radioactivity, which leaks away at a steady rate. The amount remaining helps date the fossil.

Evolution through time

332 Earth has existed for a very long time – 4600 million years. It is difficult to imagine that length of time, so it is much easier to think of it as a single day or 24 hours.

333 Millions of years passed before the first living organisms appeared on Earth. The first bacteria, formed of a single cell, arrived just before 06:00 (6 am) in the morning. That was about 3500 million years ago. The first cell with a nucleus evolved a long time later – at about 14:00 (2 pm) in the afternoon.

334 Evolution was slow at first. Several hours passed before multi-cellular organisms evolved. These are organisms formed from many cells joined together. By 19:00 (7 pm) there were seaweeds and jellyfish in the oceans. Just after 21:00 (9 pm) – about 530 million years ago – the oceans were full of life, with huge numbers of trilobites (hard-shelled, marine creatures) and other creatures.

335 Animals moved onto land and by 22:00 (10 pm) there were insects flying in the sky. The dinosaurs ruled the Earth from about 23:00 (11 pm), while the first small, furry mammals appeared soon afterwards.

EVOLUTION THROUGH TIME KEY

1 Simple cells
2 Cyanobacteria
3 Cnidarians (soft-bodied animals)
4 Ediacaran (early marine animals)
5 *Anomalocaris* (arthropod – animals with segmented bodies and no backbone)
6 Cockroach (insect)
7 Cycad (cone-bearing plant)
8 Coelacanth (fish)
9 *Diadectes* (reptile-like amphibian)
10 *Dimetrodon* (small, early reptile)
11 Plesiosaur (marine reptile)
12 *Lilienstennus* (dinosaur)
13 *Pteranodon* (flying reptile)
14 Brachiosaur (large dinosaur)
15 Magnolia (flowering plant)
16 *Archaeopteryx* (early bird)
17 *Quetzalcoatlus* (pterosaur – flying reptile)
18 *Tyrannosaurus rex* (dinosaur)
19 Moa (flightless bird)
20 *Plesiadapis* (early mammal)
21 *Indricotheres* (rhinoceros-like mammal)
22 Sabre-tooth (carnivorous mammal)
23 *Macrauchenia* (hoofed mammal)
24 Wolf (carnivorous mammal)
25 *Homo sapiens* (modern man)

▲ This diagram shows the evolution of life from the very first organisms that appeared more than 3000 million years ago to modern humans.

336 It's difficult to believe that humans have been around for a relatively short time. Modern man arrived on Earth at just one minute to midnight, about 200,000 years ago.

337 Understanding the evolutionary clock helps scientists work out the speed at which evolution takes place. Over the last 4600 million years, species have appeared and then disappeared, to be replaced by other species more suited to the changing environments.

The start of life

338 For a few hundred million years, Earth was a hot mass of molten rock and gases. The atmosphere – the layer of gases that surrounds the Earth – contained water vapour, carbon dioxide and nitrogen but no oxygen. Gradually, the surface cooled, clouds formed and water vapour fell as rain. Rain poured onto the land to create the oceans.

Frequent volcanic activity

◀ The Earth looked very different 3000 million years ago, during a period known as the Archaean. Much of the planet was covered by oceans.

339 Once there were oceans, conditions became more suited to the evolution of living things. The first building blocks of life appeared – amino acids, proteins and DNA. There are many theories about how these chemicals were created and how they joined up to form cells, but nobody knows for sure. It is one of the greatest mysteries.

Deep sea vents

Stromatolites

▼ Stromatolites, a type of cyanobacteria, are among the earliest fossils. They can still be seen at Shark Bay, Australia.

340 The cooling continued and by about 3500 million years ago the first cells had evolved. These first cells were cyanobacteria. They grew in the sunny parts of the ocean and used sunlight to make food. During this process, cyanobacteria released oxygen into the atmosphere.

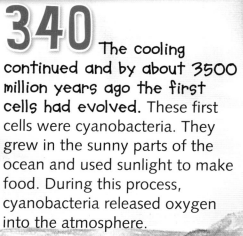

341 For the next 2500 to 3000 million years, life was very simple. There was bacteria, simple animals and plants, but no animals with a head, body and tail.

Jellyfish

▶ The first animals were soft bodied like jellyfish. *Charnia* was a strange animal that looked more like a plant.

Charnia

342 About 570 to 600 million years ago, evolution took off. Within a hundred million years or so, there were thousands of new species. There were seaweeds in the oceans, which – like the cyanobacteria – used light to make food, and there was an abundance of animals in the oceans.

Early animals

343 Fossils show that there were some very unusual animals living in the oceans about 500 million years ago. Some had several heads, trunks like elephants, backward-facing mouths, and many other odd features.

Opabinia

▼ Animals from the Cambrian Period died out when conditions on Earth changed. There are no living relatives.

Pikaia

344 Thousands of fossils have been found at the Burgess Shale deposits in Canada. The site was discovered in 1909 by Charles Walcott (1850–1927). He dug up more than 65,000 fossils. Amazingly, some were of soft-bodied animals such as jellyfish.

Ottoia

Pirania

▶ These scientists are working on a dig in the famous Walcott Quarry in the Burgess Shale deposits, Canada.

345 The oceans were full of life during the Cambrian Period (545–495 million years ago). There were molluscs, echinoderms, trilobites, worms, jellyfish and some early fish. Fish were different from the other animals as they had backbones – they were the first vertebrate animals.

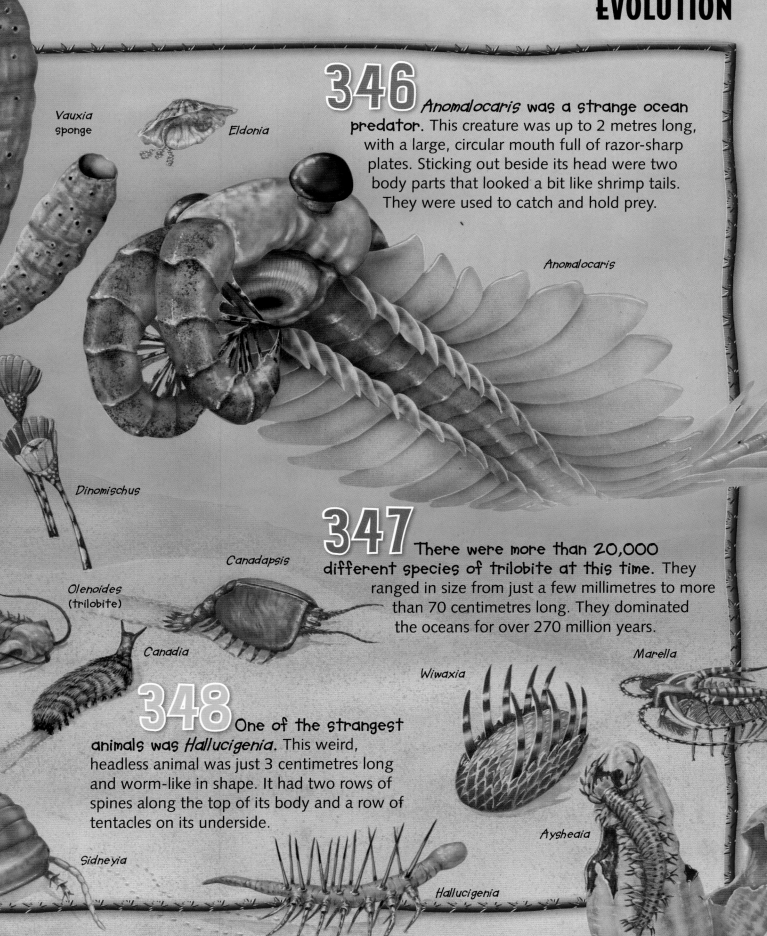

Vauxia sponge

Eldonia

346
Anomalocaris was a strange ocean predator. This creature was up to 2 metres long, with a large, circular mouth full of razor-sharp plates. Sticking out beside its head were two body parts that looked a bit like shrimp tails. They were used to catch and hold prey.

Anomalocaris

Dinomischus

Canadapsis

347
There were more than 20,000 different species of trilobite at this time. They ranged in size from just a few millimetres to more than 70 centimetres long. They dominated the oceans for over 270 million years.

Olenoides (trilobite)

Canadia

Wiwaxia

Marella

348
One of the strangest animals was *Hallucigenia*. This weird, headless animal was just 3 centimetres long and worm-like in shape. It had two rows of spines along the top of its body and a row of tentacles on its underside.

Aysheaia

Sidneyia

Hallucigenia

Moving onto land

349 Simple plants first appeared about 400 million years ago. Mosses are primitive plants that can only grow in damp areas. Ferns are more highly evolved – they appeared 350 million years ago. By around 300 million years ago much of the land was covered by conifer forests and swamps.

▲ This scene shows some early tree and plant species in a flooded forest during the Carboniferous Period (359–299 million years ago).

350 Most of the first land animals were plant eaters. One was *Arthropleura*, the largest ever millipede-like animal. Although it was related to arthropods such as insects and crabs, it grew to the size of a crocodile, with a body up to 2 metres in length.

351 Imagine a scorpion larger than you! This was *Pterygotus*, a fearsome predator that hunted fish more than 400 million years ago. Some of its relatives were among the first animals to crawl onto land. Sea scorpions are extinct, but they were the ancestors of the arachnid animal group that includes spiders and scorpions.

▼ Fossil footprints of *Arthropleura* have been found in rocks, showing the animals moved quickly over the ground.

EVOLVING ANIMALS

You will need:

pencil   notepad   tracing paper

1. Draw a simple outine of an animal.
2. Make a copy using tracing paper, but change one body part.
3. Trace the second picture. This time change something else.
4. Do this ten times, then look at your drawings to see how the animal evolved.

352 The first flying insects appeared about 350 million years ago. Scientists think that wings evolved from flaps on their main body. Insects used them to slow their fall to the ground. As the flaps got larger, the insects could glide, and then fly. The largest flying insects were ancestors of the dragonflies.

▲ The *Meganeura* dragonfly had a huge wingspan of up to one metre across, making it one of the largest ever insects to fly.

353 A few fish evolved fleshy front fins, which they used to prop themselves up on land. They flipped across sandy beaches from puddle to puddle, just like the modern mudskipper. In time, these fins developed into legs and the first four-legged vertebrates called tetrapods appeared – the amphibians.

Eusthenopteron
A lobe-finned fish that lived in muddy swamps about 385 million years ago.

Tiktaalik
This fish had limb-like fins that could support it on land.

354 Amphibian eggs dry up if they are laid on land. This meant that prehistoric amphibians always had to return to water to lay their eggs. The next big evolutionary leap came when reptiles evolved the ability to lay eggs on land.

▶ Tetrapods (four-limbed animals) such as *Icthyostega* evolved from fish over millions of years, as their bodies adapted to live on land.

Icthyostega
The limbs of this animal adapted to allow it to crawl on land.

Reptiles and dinosaurs

355 The first reptiles developed from amphibians around 315 million years ago. They were small, lizard-like animals that laid eggs with a leathery shell. This adaption meant they could live in dry habitats. They moved onto land where few animals had ventured before.

▲ One of the first reptiles was *Hylonomus*, a small, lizard-like animal. It laid eggs on land.

▲ Over millions of years, more than 1000 different dinosaur species evolved as they adapted to Earth's changing environments.

356 Dinosaurs evolved about 230 million years ago from a group of crawling reptiles. Dinosaurs ruled the Earth for about 170 million years, outnumbering the many other backboned creatures that lived at the same time.

357 The first dinosaurs, such as *Eoraptor*, were small, upright and ran on their back legs. Their upright posture was possible because they developed different hips from other reptiles. They could place their legs directly under their body to raise it off the ground. This allowed them to move faster.

358 The smallest dinosaurs weighed just a few kilograms, but there were some giants too. One of the largest was *Argentinosaurus*, which scientists think was about 40 metres long and weighed up to 50 tonnes. It is difficult to be sure as complete skeletons are rarely found.

▼ For about 100 million years enormous dinosaurs called sauropods, including *Argentinosaurus*, roamed the planet.

▶ *Giganotosaurus* was one of the largest carnivorous dinosaurs. Like *Argentinosaurus*, it lived in South America.

359 One of the most well known dinosaurs is *T rex*. It was one of the largest land carnivores that ever existed. *T rex* stood up on its hind legs and used its long tail to balance. It was 4 metres high at the hips and about 13 metres long. Despite its size, it was not quite as large as its relative *Giganotosaurus*.

▲ Near the end of the dinosaur's reign, sauropods were replaced by the plant-eating *Triceratops* (1), *Ankylosaurus* (2) and the duck-billed dinosaurs (3).

360 About 65 million years ago a huge number of living things died out in a short time. This was probably caused by a meteor smashing into Earth, throwing up vast amounts of dust into the atmosphere and causing a global winter. More than half of the world's species could not survive the sudden changes and became extinct, including nearly all large land animals.

The first birds

Bald eagle

361 About 150 million years ago a small type of dinosaur evolved feathers and the ability to fly. Many scientists believe this dinosaur became the first bird. Birds are more closely related to the dinosaurs than dinosaurs are to modern-day crocodiles because they share a common ancestor.

Talons for grabbing prey

Velociraptor

▲ *Velociraptor* had hands and feet with curved claws, similar to the talons of modern-day birds of prey.

Long tail

► Scientists are not sure whether *Archaeopteryx* could flap its wings or just glide from tree to tree.

362 Darwin suspected that birds and dinosaurs were linked. In 1861, just two years after *On the Origin of Species* was published, the fossil skeleton of a bird-like creature, *Archaeopteryx*, was discovered. It had features of both dinosaurs, such as teeth and a bony tail, and birds, such as wings.

363 Birds share many features with reptiles. Reptiles have scaly skin, and scales can still be seen on the legs of birds. Both birds and reptiles lay eggs with a shell. Birds are thought to be descended from small, raptor-like dinosaurs called 'maniraptorans', which includes the *Velociraptor*.

Long flight feathers

Lightweight body

Wing claws

Toothed beak

◄ The feathers, claws and skull of *Archaeopteryx* can be seen clearly on fossils of this prehistoric creature.

364 There are many theories to explain why dinosaurs grew feathers. Birds use feathers for flying and for signalling to each other. As dinosaurs did not have wings, the first feathers may have had a different role – to provide warmth. After the dinosaurs evolved feathers, they became coloured for communication. They were used later for flight.

Feathers

▲ Dinosaurs such as *Guanlong* may have had brightly coloured feathers to attract mates.

365 After the age of the dinosaurs, the terror birds became the biggest predators. The earliest terror birds were chicken-sized, but a much larger bird called *Phorusrhacos* evolved on the grasslands of South America. This large, ostrich-like bird was more than 3 metres tall and could run at speeds of more than 60 kilometres an hour. The last survivors died out about 5000 years ago.

▶ *Gastornis* was a fearsome predator with its crushing beak and clawed feet.

I DON'T BELIEVE IT!
The prehistoric-looking cassowary from Australia has stiff feathers and small wings. Its ancestors could fly, but over millions of years cassowaries have lost the ability to take to the sky.

366 One of the largest birds that ever lived was the huge, flightless *Gastornis*. This giant, meat-eating bird stood more than 2 metres tall. It was equipped with an amazing weapon – a large, hatchet-shaped beak. It could crush the backbone of a small horse with just one bite.

Mammals take over

367 The first mammals evolved about 220 million years ago, and existed alongside the dinosaurs. They evolved from a different group of reptiles to dinosaurs and birds, called therapsids. The first mammals were small and weasel-like, and they probably hunted insects.

▶ The small, early mammal *Leptictidium* used its long snout to sniff out prey such as this cicada.

368 The rise of mammals was not quick – it took millions of years for them to develop and become more varied. Just like the dinosaurs before them, mammals evolved to suit many different habitats. Some returned to the sea in the form of whales and dolphins, others evolved long legs and roamed the grasslands, while bats developed wings and took to the air.

369 All mammals have the same arrangement of bones in their limbs. This is called the pentadactyl limb. The basic plan in the arm is a single bone in the upper limb (the humerus), which is jointed to two bones in the lower limb (the radius and the ulna). Each limb ends in five digits.

▼ The pentadactyl limb in each of these mammals has evolved so that it is adapted to suit their lifestyle.

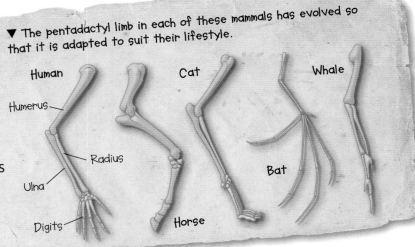

Human

Cat

Whale

Humerus

Radius

Ulna

Bat

Digits

Horse

370

Around 50 million years ago the first horse-like animal appeared – *Hyracotherium*. These forest animals were the size of dogs. When grasslands replaced the forests, animals such as *Miohippus* took over from the *Hyracotherium*. *Miohippus* had large, ridged teeth for chewing tough grasses.

▲ *Miohippus* lived from about 36 to 25 million years ago. Its fossils have been found in North America.

371

Some amazing mammals lived during the last Ice Age, about 70,000 years ago. They adapted to survive in the extreme cold, as much of the land was covered in ice. Woolly mammoths lived alongside the sabre-tooth. This big cat was more like a bear in size and hunted bison and small mammoths.

QUIZ

Which of the following mammals is the odd one out?

Tiger Seal Horse Echidna
Bat Whale Dog

Answer:
Echidna, the rest are placental mammals

372

There are almost 5500 species of mammal alive today. The most primitive are the egg-laying monotremes, such as the echidna, which share many characteristics with their reptilian ancestors. Marsupials such as the kangaroo and koala give birth to tiny babies that they care for in their pouch. The biggest group is the placental mammals, which give birth to well-developed young.

▶ Seals are placental mammals. The females are pregnant for one year and feed their young on milk.

▶ Marsupial mammals such as kangaroos carry their young around in a pouch.

▶ There are only two monotreme mammals, the echidna (right) and the duck-billed platypus.

The human story

373 Humans belong to the primate mammal group. All primates have a large brain for their size, with forward-facing eyes that give 3D vision. Most primates have fingers with nails that are used for manipulating and grasping objects.

Forward-facing eyes

Large brain

▶ Primates include lemurs, monkeys and apes such as gibbons, chimps and gorillas (shown here).

Fingers with nails

Ardipithecus ramidus
4.4 million years ago

374 The first primates appeared about 75 million years ago. Humans have a common ancestor with chimps that lived in Africa about six million years ago. Then the line splits, with chimps evolving separately to humans. Four million years ago, our human ancestors were still tree dwellers that tottered on two legs.

Australopithecus afarensis
3.9–2.9 million years ago

▶ This timeline shows how various human groups have evolved, from very early kinds that lived in Africa over four million years ago, to modern humans.

Australopithecus africanus
2–3 million years ago

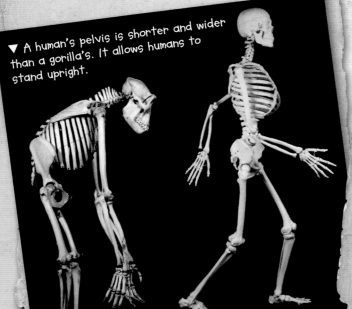

▼ A human's pelvis is shorter and wider than a gorilla's. It allows humans to stand upright.

375 Two-and-a-half million years ago, the first human ancestor to use tools appeared. *Homo habilis* had a large brain and was very adaptable. It ate a varied diet, scavenging meat rather than eating grasses and learnt to use stone tools to smash bones to get at the rich marrow inside.

376 Two million years ago, one group of early humans moved out of Africa, and populated other regions of the world. This ancestor was *Homo erectus*, and it had a more human-like appearance. It lived in a variety of different habitats and learnt how to use fire and cook food.

377 Neanderthal people lived in Europe about 130,000 years ago. Europe was still in an Ice Age at this time. The Neanderthals had a short, stocky body, which was adapted for living in the cold. They hunted animals and ate a mostly meat diet. Then about 30,000 years ago, the climate got warmer, humans from Africa arrived and the Neanderthals died out.

Homo habilis 2.5–1.4 million years ago

Homo erectus 1.8–1.3 million years ago

378 The modern human, with a highly developed brain, originated in Africa about 200,000 years ago. Like many other early humans, modern humans proved to be highly adaptable. They developed a culture and language, and learnt to depend on tools to alter their environment.

Homo sapiens neanderthalensis 150,000–30,000 years ago

Homo sapiens sapiens 200,000 to present

Designer evolution

379 People can alter evolution through artificial selection. This is similar to natural selection, but it involves people selecting the parents of the next generation. Over time, artificial selection can lead to new types of plants and animals.

380 The pet dog is related to the wolf. About 15,000 years ago, people started to tame the wolves that were found around their settlements. Over time, the appearences of the tamed animals changed as people selected parent dogs with particular features.

▼ Dogs can be grouped according to their appearance and the purpose for which they were bred.

GUNDOG
Irish setter

HOUND
Irish wolfhound

TERRIER
Jack Russell

TOY
Chihuahua

UTILITY
Bulldog

WORKING
Old English sheepdog

▲ Wolves are ancestors of all dog breeds. Wolves and dogs still have many features in common such as howling and barking.

381 The many different dog breeds look very different, but they are all the same species. This means they can breed with each other. There are different breeds of pet cats too, each bred for a particular appearance.

382 Artificial selection has developed crops and livestock too. By choosing parent plants with high yields or disease resistance, scientists have changed crop plants, such as wheat and rice. Dairy cows are now producing more milk, as farmers breed from cows that produce the most milk.

383 The most beneficial characteristics are chosen during artificial selection. Because most living things have two parents, they show variation – new features that have developed as a result of their parental genes being shuffled. This gives some individuals an advantage. For example, some plants' genes make them grow taller, allowing them to reach sunlight more easily than other plants.

384 Clones – individuals that are genetically identical to each other – can also be made by artificial selection. They are at an evolutionary disadvantage, however, because there is no variation between the individuals. If a group of cloned animals or plants are affected by disease, they could all be wiped out.

▲ Plant breeding can produce crop plants with more flavour, greater yields and more resistance to disease.

▼ Modern varieties of rice have greater yields. The latest types have been genetically altered so they survive in drought and salt water conditions.

Evolution in action

385 Evolution never stops – it is taking place around us right now. Usually, it occurs slowly, over millions of years. It took modern humans six million years to evolve from forest-dwelling animals. But sometimes evolution can happen in just a few years – or even less.

386 By understanding evolution, scientists have a better chance of fighting diseases. Humans can be vaccinated against influenza ('flu), a disease caused by a virus. The virus can evolve quickly, meaning scientists must keep developing new vaccines to keep up.

▲ Influenza vaccines no longer work when mutations change the surface of the influenza virus.

387 Farmers use weedkillers on their crops, but some weeds are becoming resistant. When a crop is sprayed, any weed that has a gene for resistance to the weedkiller survives, while the others die. This survivor produces seeds and soon there are more resistant weeds.

▼ The excessive use of weedkillers can cause some weeds to evolve a resistance to the chemicals.

▲ Mosquitoes carry parasites that cause malaria. The rise in global temperatures means they can now survive in more places.

388
The world's climate is changing and this is affecting evolution. Species with more variation can adapt to the changes and survive, while those that can't keep up are in danger of dying out. Climate change is also affecting the arrival of the seasons – in many places, spring is starting earlier. This is causing problems for plants and animals that depend on each other for survival.

389
Some lizards are changing their appearance to escape ants. Fire ants are small but aggressive and can kill the small fence lizard. Lizards that live close to these ants have longer legs than those that live in areas without the ants. Genes for long legs have been inherited to help the lizards escape.

▲ Long-legged fence lizards are more likely to survive and breed than the short-legged ones.

▼ The Hadza tribe of Africa are one of the few remaining hunter-gather tribes living in a way similar to our ancient ancestors.

390
Humans have evolved over the last few thousand years. Many adults cannot drink milk due to the lactose (sugar) it contains. About 5000 years ago, Europeans began keeping cattle. A mutation occured that allowed adults to digest the lactose. Human beings are an adaptable species – our ability to change may help us to survive in an ever-changing world.

Index

158

Acknowledgements

The publishers would like to thank the following sources for the use of their photographs:
Key: t = top, b = bottom, l = left, r = right, c = centre, bg = background

Front cover mathagraphics/Shutterstock **Spine** Johan Swanepoel/Shutterstock; Gen Epic Solutions/Shutterstock;
Back cover (clockwise from l) Lightspring/Shutterstock; David Parker/Science Photo Library; Keith Gentry/Shutterstock; Mary Clay/Ardea
Endpapers axon/Shutterstock

Alamy 50(bl) Guy Bell; 70(tr) Granger Historical Picture Archive; 73(c) Photo Researchers; 78(bl) Pictorial Press Ltd;
157(b) Ariadne Van Zandbergen

Ardea 129(cr) Piers Cavendish, (b) Mary Clay; 152(bl) Jean Michel Labat

Bridgeman Art Library 71(bl) British Library Board

Dreamstime 18(b) Silverstore; 19(br) Adam1975; 21(tr) Paha_l; 34(t) Zoom-zoom; 87(br) Alangh; 88(b) Velkol; 103(tr) Tobkatrina;
109(tr) Kati1313; 121(tr) Barsik; 131(crab) Mailthepic

FLPA 132(tr) Rob Reijnen/Minden Pictures; 133(bc), (br) Tui De Roy/Minden Pictures; 135(b) Thomas Marent/Minden Pictures;
154(c) Paul Sawer

Fotolia.com 13(tl) Paul Heasman, (cr) Dariusz Kopestynski; 21(br) photlook; 97(tl) chrisharvey; 99(cl) Alexander Yakovlev; 126(cl) &
127(cl) Kirsty Pargeter; 129(tc) Darren Hester; 137(paper bg, rt) Alexey Khromushin

Getty 39(b) Laguna Design/Oxford Scientific; 50(c) Will & Deni McIntyre; 52(br) Leemage/Universal Images Group; 57(cr) Universal
ImagesGroup; 59(tr) Jason Reed; 60(tl) Mark Ralston, (c) Barcroft Media/Contributor; 69(b) Stephen Dalton/Minden Pictures; 128(l) Anup Shah

iStockphoto.com 16–17(bg) Kevin Smith; 89(br) Rosemarie Gearhart; 141(tr) Jouke van der Meer

Louie Psihoyos 136–137(c)

NASA 56(c) NASA/JPL; 78(bg) NASA/JPL/California Institute of Technology; 79(c) NASA/JPL-Caltech; 82(tl) NASA/JPL-Caltech

Photoshot 134(c) & 136(cl) NHPA

Rex Features 81(cr) Jason Rasgon; 137(tr) KeystoneUSA-ZUMA

Science Photo Library 48(c) Anakao Press/Look at Sciences; 54(b) Christian Jegou Publiphoto Diffusion; 64(br) Sheila Terry; 67(br) Peter Menzel;
69(t) Javier Trueba; 74(bg) U.S. Navy; 77(c) Mikkel Juul Jensen, (bl) Lawrence Livermore; 78(tr) Harvard College Observatory; 83(tc) Thomas
Deerinck, NCMIR, (br) David Parker; 126–127(c) Mark Garlick; 138–139(c) Jose Antonio Peñas; 140–141(c) Christian Jegou Publiphoto Diffusion;
142(bl) Alan Sirulnikoff; 144(bg) Christian Jegou Publiphoto Diffusion; 149(b) Jaime Chirinos; 150(cr) Christian Darkin; 152–153(c) Philippe
Plailly/Eurelios; 155(cl) Philippe Psaila; 156(cl) Jose Antonio Peñas

Shutterstock.com 1 Kjpargeter; 2–3 Shilova Ekaterina; 4–5 XYZ; 6–7(bg) ssguy; 8–9(c) Sergey Lavrentev; 9(t) Ljupco Smokovski; 10(bg) Deymos,
(tr) Vakhrushev Pavel, (bl) Ivonne Wierink; 11(t) w shane Dougherty; 12(tr) yuyangc; 14(c) yxm2008, (bl) ARENA Creative; 15(br) Tatiana
Makotra; 20(bg) asharkyu, (c) Eimantas Buzas; 22–23(c) vadim kozlovsky; 24(b) Smileus; 25(cr) Ray Hub; 26(c) Sebastian Crocker; 27(br) Hywit
Dimyadi; (c) ifong; 29(tl) Viktor Gmyria; 30–31(bg) Redshinestudio; 31(tl), (cl), (bl) & (br) Annette Shaff; 32(b) Jaggat; 33(c) michael rubin;
34(tr) Maksim Toome, (cr) Balazs Toth, (r) CaptureLight, (bl) Jaochainoi; 40(tl) Kurhan, (b) Tamara Kulikova; 41(tr) Alexander Raths, (b) Kirsty
Pargeter; 43(tr) wim claes, (br) indiangypsy; 44(c) beerkoff, (bl) Smit; 47(tr) Morgan Lane Photography, (b) ssuaphotos; 48(r) kanate;
49(br) Cameramannz; 50(br) & 76(bl) happydancing; 51(b) nuttakit; 53(bg) pixeldreams.eu, (br) Maridav; 54(cr) c.; 55(tr) Janaka Dharmasena,
(bl) Suzan Oschmann; 56(bl) Olegusk; 57(l) Ana del Castillo; 58(bg) basel101658, (t) D. Kucharski & K. Kucharska, (c) Jubal Harshaw;
59(c) argus; 60(bg) Chepko Danil Vitalevich, (b) testing, (c) nuttakit; 61(b) koya979; 62(br) Gerasia, (bl) vovan, (bg) beboy; 63(bl) happydancing,
(tr) thoron; 64(bl) JonMilnes, (tr) Mazzzur; 65(bg) omer cicek, (tr, l–r) bonchan, Arturo Limon, bonchan, Denis Selivanov, (br) fzd.it;
66–67(bg) Gunnar Pippel; 66(bg) Molodec, (br) nuttakit; 68(cl) Andy Lidstone, (c) AridOcean, (b) Jason Duggan, (bl) Alfie Photography,
(br) Brandelet; 71(c) Fotocrisis; 72(c) Stephen Aaron Rees; 74(br) MrJafari, (bl) Stephen Aaron Rees; 77(b) wanchai; 80(bl) Lisa F. Young;
81(tl) Andrey Yurlov, (bl) Linda Z Ryan; 84–85(c) jan kranendonk; 84(tl) Jurgen Ziewe; 89(tl) Kozlovskaya Ksenia; 90(bl) Lilya Espinosa;
91(bl) Stanislav Fridkin; 92(tr) Jeanne Hatch, (c) Felix Mizioznikov, (cr) wong sze yuen; 93(cl) Steven Chiang, (br) Carmen Steiner;
96(bg) konmesa; 100(bl) Taranova; 101(tr) Jaren Jai Wicklund; 102(cr) JonMilnes; 105(cr) Lawrence Wee; 106–107(c) Elena Schweitzer;
106(b) Yuri Arcurs; 112–113(bg) Sebastian Kaulitzki; 115(tr) beerkoff; 117(cl) Paul Matthew Photography; 119(tl) Elena Elisseeva;
123(tr) Sebastien Burel; 124(b) picturepartners; 125(b) Monkey Business Images; 128(br) Brandelet; 130(crinoids) Rostislav Ageev,
(starfish) Christopher Elwell, (brittlestars) FAUP, (sea urchins) NatalieJean, (sea cucumbers) Philip Lange, (c, bg) kanate, (bl panel, rt) donatas1205;
131(tiger), (lion), (caracal), (domestic cat), (cheetah), (red fox), (sea lion), (gorilla), (koala) and (frog) Eric Isselée, (weasel) Ronnie Howard,
(wolf) Maxim Kulko, (bat) Kirsanov, (whale) Computer Earth, (rabbit) Stefan Petru Andronache, (polar bear) Ilya Akinshin, (sailfish) holbox,
(hummingbird) Steffen Foerster Photography, (crocodile) fivespots, (dragonfly) Subbotina Anna, (starfish) Mircea Bezergheanu, (snail) Sailorr,
(jellyfish) Khoroshunova Olga, (toad) Ultrashock, (shark) Rich Carey, (snake) fivespots, (eagle) Steve Collender, (bg) Mark Carrel,
(coloured panels, rt) sharpner; 132(c) ryadnikov Sergey, (r) Mark Bridger, (bl) Paul Broadbent, (b) U.P.images_vector; 133(cl) AridOcean,
(c) Anton Balazh, (cr) & (bl) Stubblefield Photography, (tr, rt) donatas1205; 135(bl) Anton Balazh; 136(bl) donatas1205; 139(cr) illustrart;
144–145(bg) Andre Mueller; 144(bl) & 147(bl) donatas1205; 146–147(bg) Pakhnyushcha; 148(bg) Lucy Baldwin, (tr) FloridaStock;
152–153(bg) Mark Carrel, (c) saiko3p; 155(br) Dudarev Mikhail; 156(b) Fotokostic; 157(tr) Pasi Koskela

TopFoto 58(bl), 61(c) & 66(tr) The Granger Collection; 73(tc) World History Archive

All other photographs are from: DigitalSTOCK, digitalvision, John Foxx, PhotoAlto, PhotoDisc, PhotoEssentials, PhotoPro, Stockbyte

All artworks are from the Miles Kelly Artwork Bank

Every effort has been made to acknowledge the source and copyright holder of each picture.
Miles Kelly Publishing apologizes for any unintentional errors or omissions.

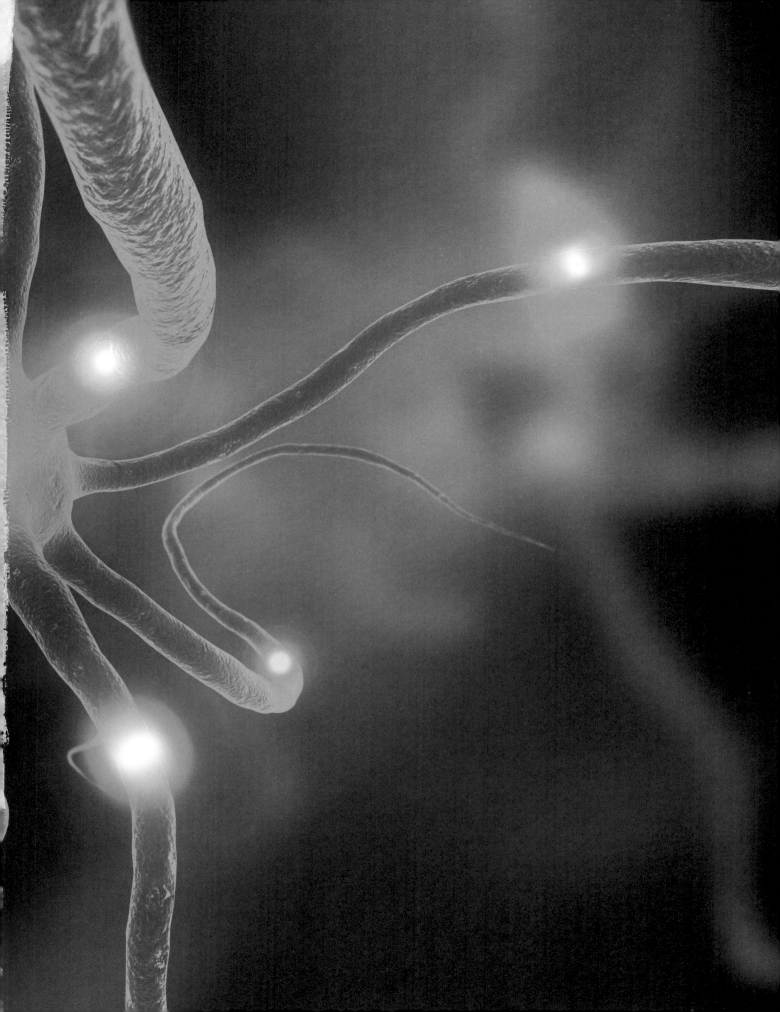

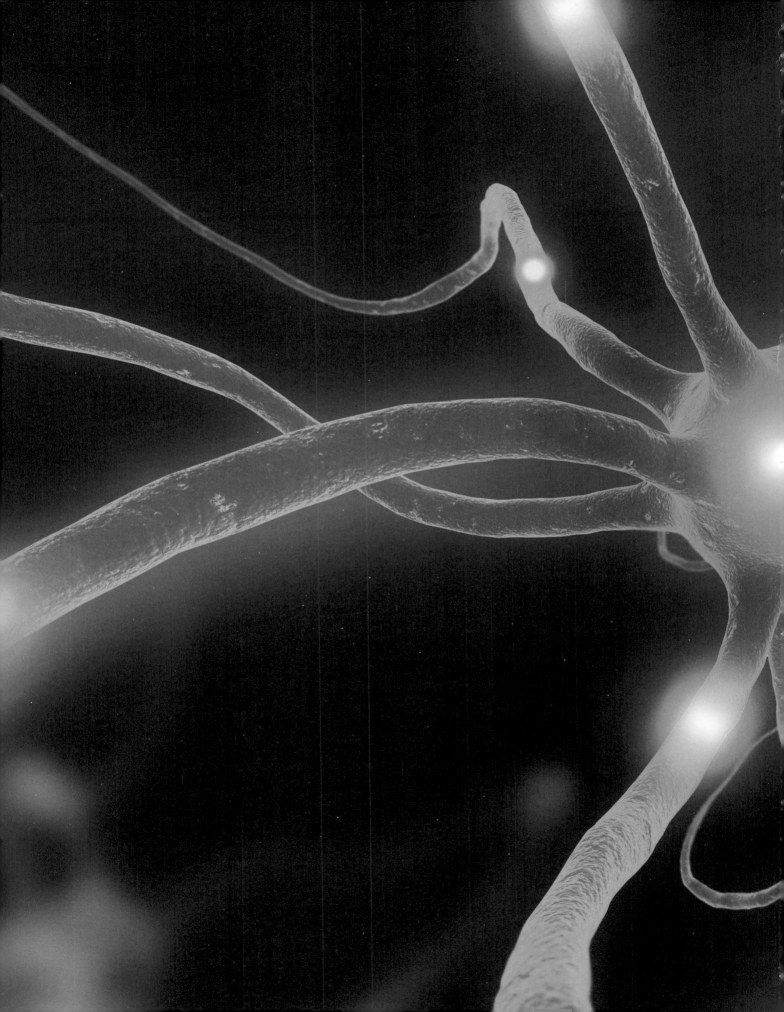